"Media create their most powerful effects when they efface evidence of their activity."
—Brian Rotman, *Becoming Beside Ourselves*

"AI, robots and humans work better when they work together. Human chess players in collaboration with AI chess programmes consistently beat both other humans and other computers working on their own."
—Klaus Schwab, *Shaping the Fourth Industrial Revolution*

"I've compared Griffith's career to the Icarus myth; but at the same time, I've never been certain whether the moral of the Icarus story should only be, as is generally accepted, 'Don't try to fly too high.' Or whether it might also be thought of as, 'Forget the wax and feathers, and do a better job on the wings.'"
—Stanley Kubrick, final speech

THE KUBRICKON

THE KUBRICKON

The Cult of Kubrick, Attention Capture, & the Inception of AI

Jasun Horsley

AEON

First published in 2023 by
Aeon Books

Copyright © 2023 by Jasun Horsley

The right of Jasun Horsley to be identified as the author of this work has been asserted in accordance with §§ 77 and 78 of the Copyright Design and Patents Act 1988.

All rights reserved. No part of this publication may be reproduced, stored in a retrieval system, or transmitted, in any form or by any means, electronic, mechanical, photocopying, recording, or otherwise, without the prior written permission of the publisher.

British Library Cataloguing in Publication Data

A C.I.P. for this book is available from the British Library

ISBN-13: 978-1-80152-056-0

Cover artwork by Jasun & Michelle Horsley
Typeset by Medlar Publishing Solutions Pvt Ltd, India

www.aeonbooks.co.uk

CONTENTS

INTRODUCTION
Confessions of a sick mind (Stanley Kubrick's Atrocity Exhibition) xi
  His hands were tied (the Kubrick vacuum) xi
  Secret pedophile elites xvi
  Culturally co-opted cognitive counterfeits xxii
  King culture xxv

PART I
THE ARCHITECTURE OF IMMERSION

CHAPTER 1
Children of Kubrick 5
  The man 6
  Deny all knowledge 8
  Immersion criticism 11
  Extraordinary facts and ridiculous flights
    of hermeneutic fantasy 14

CHAPTER 2
Full metal emperor   19
  Needful guesswork   20
  Cultural warfare   23
  The very idea of greatness, or: Stanley is as Stanley does   27
  The works of Satan   29

CHAPTER 3
Crossing the Kubrickon   37
  Under the seat   37
  The Overlook, again   40
  The "final" answer?   43
  A two-way mirror   48

PART II
AGENT STANLEY

CHAPTER 4
How the solar system was won   55
  The anomaly of Kubrick's optimistic vision of the future of man   56
  Theft as art   58
  Arthur C. Clarke's goldfish bowl   60
  KUBARK: sinister associations   66

CHAPTER 5
Clockwork conspiracy theories   73
  Some facts about Stanley   74
  Learning from The Master   77
  Agent Orange   81
  A clean-minded pornographer   82

CHAPTER 6
The lost language of the body   89
  Kubrick, DARPA, Simulmatics   89
  A computational theocracy   93
  Enter the dragon   95
  The apple of knowledge   98

PART III
KING VS KING

CHAPTER 7
The silver key — 105
   The wasp's nest — 106
   An I for an I — 109
   The writer's block — 111
   The golden Bowman — 114

CHAPTER 8
White man's burden, or: the Grand Unified Theory of
***The Shining* (GUTS)** — 119
   The axe blow — 119
   Historic trauma transmission (Sons of Saturn) — 121
   Adult boy — 125
   The secret ally — 130

CHAPTER 9
Hive mind — 139
   Word vs image — 140
   Games of thrones — 143
   Behold the para-self — 145
   DID Meets DOD: the AI breakthrough — 148

BIBLIOGRAPHY — 155

ENDNOTES — 157

INDEX — 173

INTRODUCTION

Confessions of a sick mind (Stanley Kubrick's Atrocity Exhibition)

His hands were tied (the Kubrick vacuum)

"Ludicrous from the word go."
—Pauline Kael, on *Eyes Wide Shut*[1]

This may be the first book written about Stanley Kubrick by someone who doesn't like Stanley Kubrick. Furthermore, I feel a degree of contempt for people who revere his films. Somehow, I must find a way to make this antipathy work for the subject and not against it; even if I can make it central to it. If there is a way to do this, I think it has to do with subjectivity.

Consider this a test, which is to say, an experiment. This is not a book about movies or about a famous moviemaker, but about how our perceptions around these things have been managed: how, why, and to what end. What follows is a test of the reader's Kubraphilia.

If you feel passionately about Kubrick movies, ask yourself this: who or what was the primary force that formed that passion? Taste, preference, opinion; these things are not innate to us. They are forged within us, shaped by external hands. Culture is a kind of fungus that grows inside the petri dish of the mind. But mind is like a petri dish made of the fungus that grows in it.

While this work purports to be about a big subject—the harvesting of human consciousness and life force and the creation of a form of artificial intelligence indistinguishable from demonic possession—it is, like all grandiose endeavors, rooted in the mundane and the personal, even the trivial. For example, my utter incomprehension that Kubrick's last movie, *Eyes Wide Shut*, is now almost *de rigueur* described as "Stanley Kubrick's masterpiece." That I find this fact supremely alienating might seem strange in 2023, as most of the world seems to have lost its ability to distinguish between a scientistic tyranny conducting corporate-medical experimentation and a sincere attempt to stop a pandemic using the scientific method. Sometimes, it is the smallest splinters that are the hardest to remove.

It's my view that *Eyes Wide Shut* is the product of a sick mind, in more ways than one. A sick mind as in a mind twisted by over-exposure to a world of absolute power and corruption, and a mind sick with worry that knew it was powerless to do anything about it. (According to Kubrick biographer John Baxter, "Kubrick had an absolute phobia about any stranger who approaches him. He worries constantly about being kidnapped and about his family's safety," p. 286.)

To my own mind, the only good thing about *Eyes Wide Shut* is the subtext. That's it. As a work of "art"—a cultural piece of entertainment—the only thing it has going for it is what it might be *trying to communicate*. The means of communication are so ludicrous, however, that they approach the grotesque. If *A Clockwork Orange* indicates a pathological psyche at work (Kubrick's), *Eyes Wide Shut* shows that psyche's total and final possession by pathology. Are you feeling rankled yet?

Eyes Wide Shut is a travesty. If there were such a thing as aesthetic crime, it would be guilty on almost every count. It is an erotic thriller completely devoid of erotic charge, thrills, or menace. Every scene is atrocious; the only question is: is it deliberately awful, and, if so, how and why did Kubrick achieve these effects? Is the total implausibility of every last scene—it seeming to exist in a netherworld where no recognizable form of human behavior exists—designed to simulate a dream reality? If so, it fails utterly because although it does create a feeling of excruciating discomfort, the discomfort is for Kubrick and the film itself, not for any of the characters in the movie.[2]

INTRODUCTION   xiii

But perhaps this too is deliberate. One thing I will be exploring in this work is the idea that Kubrick *wanted to make the worst film he could make as a kind of message*. This then raises the question: a message to whom, and what was it saying?

* * *

"It really is a creepily bad movie."
—Pauline Kael, on *Eyes Wide Shut*

I have seen *Eyes Wide Shut* four times now, more times than any other film I mostly detest. The reason is simple: fascination. The film holds a fascination for me, one that it did even before it began to be taken seriously by otherwise sane people (when it was first released, few people tried to defend it). The fascination it holds is born from the lurking sense that the awfulness of the film is not the usual kind of awfulness but a mysteriously *intentional* awfulness, with some awful, mysterious purpose behind it.

For many, the film holds a similar fascination—even if they don't admit to the film's awfulness—one that has to do with a feeling that Kubrick was trying to communicate something with his last movie, that his hands were somehow tied, that the film was taken away from him, and that he was killed because of it, and so on. These last two beliefs are mutually dependent.

The idea that Kubrick was killed because of *Eyes Wide Shut* (I keep typing *Eyes Wide Shit* and having to go back and correct it, reluctantly), at least the versions released in 1999, is clearly ridiculous. Despite the internet buzz around it, and a number of straw-clutching pseudo-academic essays, the film reveals nothing much about anything. As an exposé of the depraved inner workings of the elite, it's on a par with … what? … I would have to dredge my memory for the lowest grade B-movie to come up with a comparison. Why serious-minded researchers take the movie seriously at that level can only be explained by one fact: it was made by Kubrick, and Kubrick must have *known something*, because he was Kubrick. Hence the idea that he was killed to prevent the real, uncensored version of the film from ever being seen had to be invented.

I find this idea almost, but not quite, as implausible as I find *Eyes Wide Shut* implausible. I agree that Kubrick was trying to communicate *something* with *Eyes Wide Shut*, because there's no other reason to make a movie besides trying to communicate something. I would also agree that his hands were tied in some way, and that he had to make it within some very restricting limits of "decorum"—perhaps because his daughter was hostage to the Church of Scientology, which fact seems strangely entangled with Kubrick's otherwise confounding choice of Tom Cruise and Nicole Kidman for the leads in the film. Cruise was at the time Scientology's once and future celebrity king, but by the time filming began on *Eyes Wide Shut*, in November 1996, the two had been estranged from the Church for several years. Scientology chief David Miscavige had already been recruiting all of Cruise's household employees, including Michael Doven (who spied on him for ten years on behalf of the Church) to keep Miscavige up to speed on the Cruiser. *Eyes Wide Shut* "infuriated Miscavige" because "he was no longer receiving these daily reports on Cruise"; the 15-month-long shoot in the UK, including 46 straight weeks of filming (a Guinness world record), caused an extended "blackout period" for Miscavige.[3] Is it any wonder if Scientology was keen to get its hooks into Kubrick's daughter Vivian? Hostage for hostage?

Or perhaps all this was part of a larger and much older plot to control Kubrick and his movies, a plot in which abducting his daughter was only the latest move on a socio-cultural-political chessboard, with Kubrick as both King of his own petty domain and pawn within a much larger and more complex game. Whatever the behind-the-scenes story, none of it actually changes what is there on the screen (though it can change our experience of it).

Eyes Wide Shut isn't a bad film in the way *Full Metal Jacket* is a bad film—sort of forced and overwrought but lacking a movie at its center. Nor is it morally repugnant the way *A Clockwork Orange* is morally repugnant. It's significantly worse a film than either of these films, but it's also different. In *Full Metal Jacket*, it was easy to see where Kubrick was aiming for greatness and missed. With *Eyes Wide Shut*, it's hard to see *what* Kubrick was aiming for. It appears to be a kind of nightmare comedy, *à la After Hours* or David Lynch, and for the first hour of the film he *almost* pulls it off. But just at the point when it needs to go deep and dark—when Harford enters the labyrinth and becomes a live witness to the workings of the human unconscious, in all its seamy sordid glory—the film does a belly flop, and all the wind goes out of its sails. It never recovers after that. There is absolutely no tension in these later scenes; there's also no real evidence that Kubrick meant there to be. By this point, there's no way to mistake the film for a nightmarish comedy either.

Watching *Eyes Wide Shut* the last time—for what I sincerely prayed would be the last time in my life—I got the sense that Kubrick had written the script (with Frederic Raphael) and then done a William Burroughs/Brion Gysin on it, shuffled all the scenes, even the lines, into a random sequence, and then gone blindly along with whatever came up, hoping for the best. The movie *is* like a bad dream, in the worst possible sense. It is incoherent, rambling, banal, utterly implausible, and faintly embarrassing once it is over. In a word, "ludicrous" from the word go. It is like something we don't want to talk about with anyone, and would rather just forget all about.

Despite this—or because of it—people *do* want to talk about it and what it "means." Yet besides Slavoj Žižek (who explored the theme of female sexuality being an annihilating threat to the male psyche, which accounted for the total lack of *eros* in the orgy scenes[4]), no one, as far as I know, has got close to its meaning. The reason is that, as with *A Clockwork Orange*, *Eyes Wide Shut* has all the symptoms of the disease it is diagnosing. Studying it is like asking to be projectile vomited on by an Ebola case to analyze the data. All you want to do after is jump in the shower and get yourself checked out as soon as possible.

What if, with *Eyes Wide Shut*, Kubrick set out to make a movie that would be unsatisfying dramatically and aesthetically but at the same time so intriguing that we would *recreate* it in our own psyches as a way to try and *make* it work? "The film has great potential," we come away saying to ourselves, and it has some kind of weird vision. At the same time, it's over-acted, badly staged, and the dialogue is poorly written—everything about it is somehow *off*. What's more, there's nothing cathartic in *Eyes Wide Shut*; none of the scenes give us any kind of release. We can't have a natural response to them because, aesthetically and dramatically, *they're not allowing us to suspend our disbelief*.

As a result, some viewers may find they're experiencing the film on two levels: on one, something's going on here that's meaningful; on the other, they feel repulsed by it. Like Kubrick, they want to do another take, and another, over and over in their minds, to somehow make it right. So they go away and unconsciously reshoot the movie in their heads. In the film, Tom Cruise has a wild and crazy night and then spends the rest of the movie retracing his steps and trying to figure out what happened. In the same way, we may end up replaying the movie, looking for the clues that could solve the mystery and set us free from the dream narrative. Before we know it, the film has taken up permanent residence in our unconscious minds.

This is similar to why emojis are necessary when we are texting and emailing people. If all we have are the words, there's an absence of emotional meaning. Over millennia, we've become used to body language, and suddenly, in the past few decades, it's not there anymore; facial expressions and tone of voice are not there. We can't help but unconsciously fill in those spaces based on the text, and since the text is inherently cold we tend to imagine the worst. The solution is to fill it in with something friendly, something warm, something "human." A smilie!

In a similar way, a Kubrick film is emotionally cold, removed, and weirdly lifeless; it's an automatic reaction to try to animate it and make it human, to put our own blood *into* it. The movie lures us in with the promise of a movie experience, but to have one we end up actually animating it, viewing it in such a way that we give it part of our essence. In this way, the medium (machine) is *sucking the blood out of us to animate itself*. Kubrick films—like all movies, only more so—are empty vessels to be filled by the subjective lives of the audience. This is analogous, as we shall see, to AI's "need" to develop *a subjective core of sentience*.

Secret pedophile elites

> "Kubrick has indeed always had a pronounced interest in altered states of consciousness and multiple personalities."
> —Laurent Vachaud, "The Secret of the Pyramid"

One clear example of the vacuum at the core of *Eyes Wide Shut* is that of the mansion orgy scene. The message of *Eyes Wide Shut* regarding the sinister rituals of the cryptocratic elite is (in the words of Ziegler): "Nothing happened." Though we are meant to doubt the truth of this along with Harford, it is still the message of the film, because it is what we have seen for ourselves.

We have been inside the secret mansion and what we have seen, though shot in the sumptuous Kubrick style, is a great big nothing burger: a bunch of naked women and tuxedoed men having sex in kinky masks. (Kael called it "the most hygienic thing I have ever seen."[5]) In the post-Jimmy Savile, post-Jeffrey Epstein world, this shouldn't even pass for "conspiracy-lite." It's a whitewash that's also hogwash. Instead, the film is now touted all over the internet as exposing the dark underbelly of elite society, not because of what's in it, but because of the awareness that audiences bring to it and *retroactively project onto it*.

Not that it is necessarily all projection. Kubrick was an insider, so it stands to reason that his orgy scene was really a place-keeper for something far darker. Jay Weidner has suggested that, as originally intended, Harford's wife, Nicole Kidman, would have been at the masked ball as one of the sex slaves. Laurent Vachaud has pointed out that the two old men in the toy store at the end of the film are seen at Ziegler's party at the start, and that they are there in the store to kidnap the Harford daughter and turn her into a sex slave for the elites, like her mother.

These possibilities suggest a very different movie, one that would be worth discussing seriously as a chilling portrait of institutional, ritual abuse, mind control, pedophilia, etc. But this is not the movie we got, and any discussion of the film that doesn't begin with an acknowledgment of the aesthetic reality ignores the most important fact of all. It's like trying to discuss the horizon with the hoodwinked or what's outside Plato's cave with shadow-gazers.

Laurent Vachaud's "The Secret of the Pyramid" appeared in the January 2013 issue of the film journal *Positif*. His analysis was reproduced, with some oversimplified and over-literal imagery, in a YouTube video by "Gasface" and given the hard-sell and easy-to-dismiss title of "Kubrick & the Illuminati." This made it easier for one writer, in a derisive piece, to use it as an example of "the paranoid style" (a term he got from Richard Hofstadter).[6]

Vachaud's interpretation is quite speculative and overly dependent on some questionable source material (Cathy O'Brien's *Trance Formation of America*) and the conspiracy lore of mind-control "Monarchs," an unsubstantiated area of the much more firmly established MKULTRA program history. But it contains a number of observational gems. The prestigious New York-based arts magazine *Blouin ArtInfo* gave a concise summation:

> After analyzing the omnipresence of triangle patterns in the film's sets, Vachaud ... concluded that *Eyes Wide Shut* ... is about mind control exerted by the secret society to which Alice Harford (Nicole Kidman) belongs. Her husband, Bill Harford (Tom Cruise), with "big closed eyes," is blind to the fact that his wife is part of a cult

that provides sex slaves to wealthy elites. [Vachaud claims] that the theme of abused children is at the heart of all Kubrick's movies since *Lolita*, and that the Harfords' child would also become, under the control of her mother, a slave of the secret society.[7]

Central to Vachaud's thesis is the following claim from "The Secret of The Pyramid" (trans. Debra Gray and Jasun Horsley):

> Alice's strange dreams and altered states resemble a perfect Monarch victim. It is just as if Kubrick took Schniztler's novel *Traumnovelle* and changed it gradually to "Trauma-Novelle," sneaking in the theme of mind control so dear to him. In this way, everything that happens within Schnitzler's dream in the movie becomes *the fragmented memories of an alter ego*. This idea is especially clear in a scene where Bill returns home to find his wife waking from a dream, similar in many ways to his own evening in Somerton. In Kubrick's version, it is not so much a case of coincidence or "synchronicity" between Bill's experience and Alice's "dream," as of a young woman who served as a brainwashed sex slave during the ritual that Bill surprised at the castle. Alice's mind then repressed the traumatic memory so she could continue to function freely, in a reflex psychiatrists describe as a fugue state. Thus, each of the traumas suffered corresponds to a fugue state or different personality, stored in her body and brain.[8]

Certainly, this reading transforms *Eyes Wide Shut* into a much more disturbing and intriguing movie than what most people saw, not least because it provides a context for the grotesquely affected and unnatural quality of many of the scenes (besides that of Kubrick simply being out of touch with human speech patterns, dialogue, or dramatic pacing). In other words, were some of the scenes in *Eyes Wide Shut* deliberately ludicrous, or are Kubrick defenders clutching for straws and finding them in the circular eddies of pop conspiracy lore?

To support his thesis, Vachaud makes a series of observations, ranging from the tenuous to the compelling, including the following:

- Everyone in *Eyes Wide Shut* (especially Nicole Kidman) seems to be moving and speaking in a kind of daze or hypnotic trance state. (I would add, to an almost maddening degree.)

- "Throughout *Eyes Wide Shut*, Kubrick also ceaselessly forged links between Alice and the girls of the orgy." (Possibly.)
- "At Ziegler's party, Alice flees Nightingale (Todd Field) because she unconsciously recognizes the man playing the piano in Somerton." (Maybe; Alice does leave the dance floor pretty rapidly after her husband points Nightingale out to her as an old college friend, and she ignores Bill's suggestion of saying hello to him.)
- All the women Bill meets in his night-prowl represent aspects of Alice—or "alters." (Unverifiable, but a compelling reading consistent with film analysis.)
- The daughter of the costume shop owner being pimped out by her father is meant as a nod to the truth about Alice, that she is a "Monarch" sex slave. (Plausible.)
- The repeat reference to rainbows is a reference to *The Wizard of Oz* and thence to theosophy (the author of *Wizard* was a theosophist) and to cult mind control. (Plausible.)
- "The theme of childhood abuse has always been at the heart of Kubrick's work." (Debatable.)
- Kubrick's AI is the "idea of a synthetic child and his association with an android prostitute ('Gigolo Joe'), clearly suggesting what use Kubrick reserved for 'Supertoys,' the child-robots of the future." (Intriguing.)
- "In *Eyes Wide Shut*, abused childhood is everywhere." (Vachaud's hammer has started seeing nails in every frame.)
- Bill and Alice's daughter, Helena (a nod to Theosophy-founder H. P. Blavatsky?) is first seen wearing butterfly wings. (True.) "MONARCH owes its name to a variety of butterfly." (So goes the lore.)
- "At the end of the film, Helena wanders into a toy store where a game with a red logo, 'Magic Circle,' is clearly visible." (True.)
- This is followed by a shot of lots of teddy bears, "which in the United States are a well-known symbol of child abuse." (It is certainly not a well-known one. An internet search brings up a 4chan meme called "pedobear" but that began in 2010.)
- "When Helena finds the toy of her dreams in the store, it is a Barbie doll adorned with butterfly wings which she proudly brandishes in front of her parents." (True.)
- In *The Shining*, When Danny first sees the ghosts of the twin sisters at the Overlook, there is an advertising poster for a ski resort behind them, bearing the name MONARCH. (True. There is also an odd

light *shining* next to the skier's face, giving the image an extra *je ne sais quoi*. Oh, and the red fire bell echoes HAL's one red eye.)

- The event that kick starts the film's action is Alice's relaying of her encounter with the naval officer in the elevator of a hotel, in which *one glance from him* so transfixed her that she was ready to leave everything for one night with him. This suggests the effect of a post-hypnotic trigger, including a trance state or the activation of a pre-programmed "alter," *à la* MKULTRA. (Of all the plot details Vachaud samples, this is among the most compelling in terms of his thesis.)
- The father of Scientology, L. Ron Hubbard, was a naval officer. (True.)
- "Ziegler's secretary in the film is also performed by Michael Doven, a notorious Scientologist who was the 'watcher' of Cruise and features in the credits of all his films." (Not all, but certainly many. He started out as Cruise's personal assistant on *Far and Away*.)

- Vivian Kubrick joined the Church of Scientology shortly before *Eyes Wide Shut* began filming. (She did join the Church, but when exactly is unknown. Vachaud doesn't make it clear, but presumably he is implying that Kubrick's making *Eyes Wide Shut* led the Church to abduct his daughter, since he would already have been in preproduction by the time she joined. One possible implication is that Kubrick's casting of Cruise was part of a yet-to-be-declared "war on Scientology" that became official a few years later, via Anonymous, the online ARGs and IRL protests. Anonymous was a forerunner to QAnon.)

Vachaud calls *Eyes Wide Shut* "a father's requiem for his lost daughter." The *Blouin ArtInfo* article claims that

> Uncovering "barely veiled allusions" to Scientology in *Eyes Wide Shut* (among them the fact that Tom Cruise is himself a zealous Scientologist), the article claimed to discover a parallel between the movie and Kubrick's personal life. His daughter Vivian Kubrick ... joined the Scientologists during the preparation for *Eyes Wide Shut* and was no longer speaking to her family as of 1998. [I]n the last scene of *Eyes Wide Shut*, when the Harfords discuss their marriage in a toy store, their daughter seems to be kidnapped in a disturbing scene in the background. Indeed, one of the film's last images shows the child at the end of a store aisle surrounded by three men. Vachaud points out that they were already present early in the movie at the party thrown by Victor Ziegler (Sydney Pollack), an influential member of the secret society that Tom Cruise discovers. The cult thus seems to be shadowing the Harford family, and it's possible that the daughter will be kidnapped by them—another echo of Vivian Kubrick's fate, since she disappeared after becoming a Scientologist.[9]

These are not threads that I plan to pursue directly in what follows, but they do serve to indicate two things: firstly, that *Eyes Wide Shut*, independently of its merits as a movie, contains a hidden body of meanings, even an alternate *raison d'être*, or reason for being made. Secondly, this alternate reading of the film need not have anything to do with the one that has, in the two decades since its release, subsequently been attributed to it. This is central to the thesis of *The Kubrickon*: that not only are Kubrick's movies not what they seem, but they are also not what a growing consensus of Kubrick revisionists claim they are. This, I will argue, is only a deeper, darker level of seeming, a second matrix.

Culturally co-opted cognitive counterfeits

> "The ideal subject of totalitarian rule is not the convinced Nazi or the convinced Communist, but people for whom the distinction between fact and fiction (i.e., the reality of experience) and the distinction between true and false (i.e., the standards of thought) no longer exist."
> —Hannah Arendt, *The Origins of Totalitarianism*

In the last stages of writing this book, while reading some recent studies of Kubrick (Benson, and Kolker and Abrams), I had the sudden strong impression that watching Kubrick movies must cause a form of cognitive impairment. This could—and maybe should—be said of movies and TV in general. But in the case of Kubrick, I think it is considerably more observable, as being caused by a combination of the movies themselves with a decades-long PR campaign.

This may be a central clue to *The Kubrickon*: all of Kubrick's films, from *2001: A Space Odyssey* to *Eyes Wide Shut*, took time, sometimes a very long time (*The Shining, Eyes Wide Shut*) to be regarded as something other than artistic failures. This means that, besides time, they also required multiple viewings. Most of the viewers doing the revaluating—and the multiple viewing—have been the film critics, film theorists, and film-*makers* who make up the cultural vanguard of the Kubrick canonization process. In the words of (two prime suspects) Kolker and Abrams: "The commonplace about Kubrick films is that they do not fare well on first sight ... The fact is that all of Kubrick's films require more than one viewing" (p. 133).

This curious fact is invariably used, by these same reevaluators, as evidence that Kubrick was ahead of his time and of a different order of artistic intelligence, and that therefore his films require an unusual degree of acumen to understand. This trained acumen and eye is to be developed over time *through repeated exposure to the works themselves*. In other words, simple-minded viewers and critics have to be re-educated (aesthetically corrected) in order to grok Kubrick's genius, and this can only happen via a combination of rewatching the movies themselves with a close and respectful reading of the critical and academic appraisals, to be provided by trained and discerning minds.

"The more they are seen," write Kolker and Abrams, "the deeper they burrow into the unconscious, the more they become templates for our judging of other films, or even seeing the world around us. They also become fodder for a variety of interpretations, from initial reviews to scholarly readings, to conspiracy theories" (p. 133). Needless to say, the authors champion the scholarly theories while scorning the conspiracy ones. And, like Leonard Nimoy in *Invasion of the Body Snatchers*, reassuring the humans about to be replaced that they will be happier when their humanity has been expunged, they view this process of unconscious-burrowing as *unequivocally benign*.

This work will beg to differ. It's fairly well-known that both heroin and cigarettes also take a few tries to override the body's natural rejection of them so we can start to "enjoy" their effects (become addicts). The entire notion of movies requiring multiple viewings in order to acclimatize our psyches to their meanings is evidence that cultural bondage, and spiritual degradation, is at work. When human psyches need to be "adjusted"—reconfigured and reprogrammed—to be made more compatible with the strange new media they are being spliced to, then it should be apparent that something unwholesome and unnatural—if not actively diabolical—is at work.

Filming *Eyes Wide Shut* took a year and a half and involved the anally obsessive immersion of dozens of employees in the smallest and most trivial details of film décor, to a degree that was excessive even for Kubrick. And it was all to create a *mise-en-scène* as profoundly unnatural as Kubrick could achieve ("dreamlike" being the cover for dissociated and disconnected from any natural human experience). The multiple takes, according to Kolker and Abrams, "demanded that [the actors] wear down any reticence and spontaneity. The 'safe space' was only safe from the vagaries of a 'natural' or realistic performance" (Kolker and Abrams, p. 97).

Sydney Pollock's performance—besides that of Alan Cumming as a simpering homosexual hotel clerk—is possibly the most grotesque in a film populated by grotesque performances, and Pollock acknowledged his own difficulty submitting to the Master's demands:

he wanted something very special in that movie and I ... personally had trouble doing it. I did it because it was what he wanted, which was a kind of theatricality, not absolutely real like you and I are talking now. He wanted a kind of theater ... I wanted to do it but I didn't know how to do it and not be artificial. But I did shut up and do exactly what he said.

(Kolker and Abrams, p. 98)

And what Stanley demanded above all was *inauthenticity*. The same inauthenticity that the film would eventually be praised for. Evil, be thou my good.

Eyes Wide Shut may be the perfect pop cultural/high art exemplar of the madness of (post-)modern academia, and the increasingly deranged contortions it inflicts upon its adherents. I refer (in passing) to the *de rigueur* cultural mindset that has recently peaked—in the US especially—with Critical Race Theory's sustained assault on reality, in the interests of social equity. (2 + 2 = 4 is patriarchal oppression; all white people are born racist; determining the sex of a child by its genitalia is transphobic; etc.)

Simply put, those critics who admire *Eyes Wide Shut* and who argue for its artistic superiority, using a combination of convoluted sentences and outright lunacy (such as the BFI pocket book's claim that it is "the best acted film in Kubrick's work and one of the best-acted films in the entire history of cinema," Kolker and Abrams, p. 140), these are the same sort of people who create culturally co-opted cognitive counterfeits of reality like CRT curriculums. The idea, for example (Kolker and Abrams again), that *Eyes Wide Shut* is about "money, the accumulation of capital and power ... the inequality of wealth" (pp. 140, 141) can only exist in a reality-void that ignores the fact that at least four of the main crew of the film (Kubrick, Cruise, Kidman, and Pollock) were themselves obscenely wealthy capitalists (Kubrick even lived in an English mansion); only lifetime academics are capable of this sort of doublethink, though to be fair, they have done an impressive job infecting entire generations with the same cognitive disorder.[10]

The exclusion of popular creative artists from the despised "1%," for example, is one of the most glaring deficiencies in the supposed political consciousness of younger generations. It is also the most compelling evidence of the insidious power of the entertainment industry.

King culture

> "We'll know our disinformation program is complete when everything the American public believes is false."
> —William Casey, CIA Director from 1981 to 1987

The idea that Stanley Kubrick—the most established and revered filmmaker in history—was a whistleblower who died trying to expose high-level government crimes is, to me, on par with believing Donald Trump is an outsider come to "drain the swamp" of deep state pedophiles and make America great again. These emperors have no clothes, and the psy-op of superculture means to keep us hallucinating that they do, to keep us believing that, somehow, the same forces, players, principles, institutions, and values that stripped us of our autonomy, purpose, and freedom have miraculously changed their spots and, rather than devour us, are here to set us free.

Throughout history, monarchs have deployed secret armies to work day and night to preempt any potential uprisings, by creating their own resistance movements to recruit all dissidents. This is the oldest con in the book, and the proof is that all these apparent oppositions have not been mercilessly crushed into non-existence but allowed to thrive. Because if there is one thing that state power knows how to do, it is to mercilessly crush resistance.

Culture is the King behind the king. It demands never-ending worship and obeisance, the energy of attention and belief of the crowd. Controlled oppositions that offer up false saviors can even be superficially effective—enough even for the savior figures to be elected (DT)—because this only reifies the cultural and social structures and values that have birthed and anointed the new king. Since the king is only a figurehead for "state power," it matters little who they are, provided their ever-changing image is sufficiently convincing to keep the hope for a savior alive, and to perpetuate slavish dependence on external forms of authority and meaning.

Emperors come and go. Their invisible clothes, the hallucinations of the crowd, can morph and mutate to keep abreast of the times. But what must never change is the hypnotic hold of the spell being cast. The aim of this little book is to help to break that spell.

Whether it is QAnon or the cult of Kubrick, the proof that these apparently subversive movements conceal a fundamental allegiance to power is in the pudding of their cultural continuity and clout. They prevail, luring millions into virtual cathedrals of consternation, but however much the pieces on the chessboard move around, the rules of the game remain the same. All of the motions of defiance and signals of virtue change nothing, unless it be to multiply the many heads of the Hydra, and to deepen the layers of deception, in world that has been pulled over our eyes to keep us blind.

Within a larger cultural context, the cognitive impairment that I believe over-exposure to the Kubrick canon causes might be called "propaganda derangement syndrome." This is what happens after sustained, generational exposure to corporate media designed to distort reality (often in the form of entertainment) and to disconnect audience members from their own felt sense of what is true and false, until they can no longer discern the difference.

This has become more and more obvious with US election campaigns and their aftermath, as provably corrupt leaders like Barack Obama, Hillary Clinton, and Donald Trump are worshipped as paragons of virtue and society's saviors. In the case of Kubrick, it is less easy to prove the corruption of an artist ostensibly working to create works of art as a way to convey personal obsessions and concerns. I believe it *is* observable in the movies themselves (most especially *2001* and *A Clockwork Orange*), but much more so in the attempts of both Kubrick and the arts culture (especially US and UK arts) to deify the works—and the man behind them—beyond criticism.

This cultural effort has been so successful that it is now largely unrecognized, which is, paradoxically, its own kind of evidence. Pauline Kael's efforts notwithstanding, there really aren't *any* sustained counterarguments out there, when it comes to the cult of the Kubrick genius. Presumably, this is because, a) those who don't admire his works don't belong to, or in, that world; b) those who do belong there, namely, aspiring or even successful film writers and artists, know by now that to make a case against King Stanley is to risk losing credibility, while barely leaving a dent in the naked emperor's imagistic armor.

One of the premises of this book is that anything a decadent, corrupt, and at base anti-life culture, while it may have many of the outer features of goodness, cannot by definition be "good." Satan himself knows how to appear as an angel of light. All of this *should* be obvious, but it isn't. Hope that is continuously upgraded, refurbished, renewed, and injected with fresh streams of delusion, like ever deadlier booster shots for a toxic vaccine, springs eternal and infernal. How and why this diabolic process of consciousness-co-opting unfolds is the subject of *The Kubrickon*: the creation of audience cults as means to quash spontaneous awakenings within the collective psyche, and redirect their energy and attention into cunningly and cynically pre-fabricated structures of belief, or memeplexes. The process is twofold: 1) to animate and inform those structures and give them wings; 2) to co-opt the awakening and confine it to rapidly adapting, corporate-sponsored dream scenarios (*traumnovelle*). The result is singularly insistent: the dream of an awakening that forever supplants an awakening from the dream.

The strange and beguiling (and maddening) phenomenon of Kubrick-caused cognitive impairment might be fittingly compared to LSD (fitting, since Kubrick's Magnum Opus, *2001*, was sold as "the ultimate trip" to the LSD counterculture). Those who drop acid in large and/or frequent doses cannot distinguish between the impairment of their faculties and the benefits they claim it had for them. They become, in their own estimation, the proof: "Look what it did for *me*!" they cry, blissfully unaware of their wild, staring eyes, drooling mouths, and jittering bodies. They conflate disembodied derangement with religious revelation. They are using senses that have been compromised to testify to the substance that has compromised them—rather like a victim of Communist brainwashing praising Communism, unaware that what they are really testifying to is the power of brainwashing. (To be fair, it is not either/or, in any of these cases.)

The insight that Kubrick's films cause cognitive impairment—if insight it is—came late in the day to me. And although I think it is central to this book's premise (that of the harvesting of human sentience for the seeding of machine intelligence), I won't be attempting to argue it (much) in what follows. That Kubrick and his films are worth studying is the one thing this book has in common with all the other books about Kubrick, every last one of which is written by a devotee, as Stanley made sure.

It is also perhaps the only thing.

PART I

THE ARCHITECTURE OF IMMERSION

"Include utter banalities."
—Stanley Kubrick (from a notebook, regarding *Full Metal Jacket*)

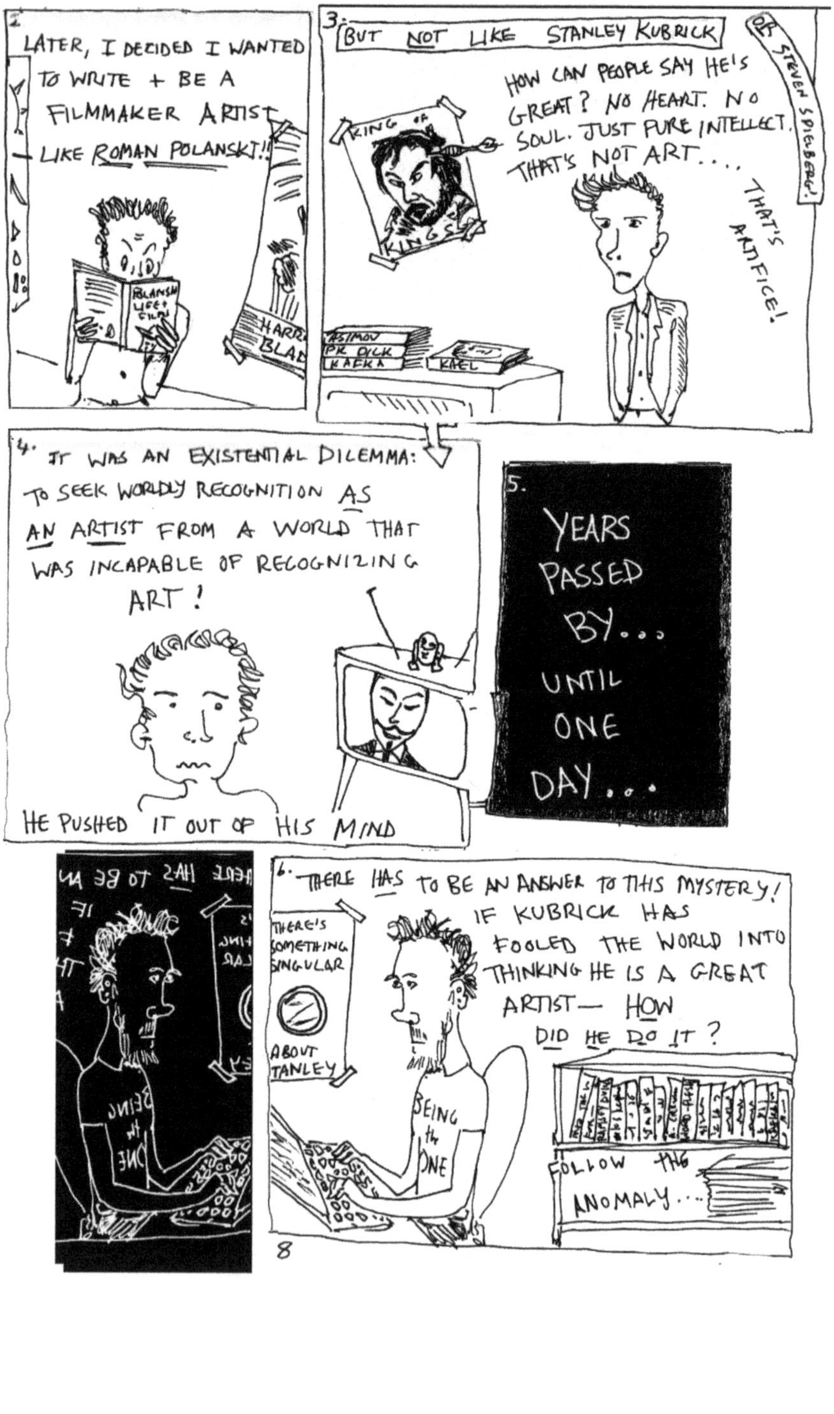

CHAPTER 1

Children of Kubrick

"We're all children of Stanley Kubrick, aren't we? Is there anything you can do that he hasn't already done?"
—Paul Thomas Anderson

In the opening credits of *2001: A Space Odyssey*, as the celestial bodies roll into alignment and as the magisterial tones of Strauss' "Thus Spoke Zarathustra" reach a crescendo, the words *"A Stanley Kubrick Production"* appear on the screen, the planets and sun lined up behind them.

Could such a bald-faced show of directorial arrogance be meant as a joke? Since there's no indication that much in *2001* is meant as a joke, apparently it was a case of self-regard taken all the way to the infinite, and beyond. (The title "Beyond the infinite" toward the end of the movie might also be seen as a joke—Kubrick's vision is so grandiose that not even infinity can contain it.) Even the Kubrick eulogists (are there any other kind of Kubrick commentators?) admit that he took nothing so seriously than the question of artistic credit. Kubrick went to great lengths to diminish Terry Southern's contribution to *Dr. Strangelove*. He refused to give "Moonwatcher" Dan Richter full credit on *2001*, wanting to be the only name in the credits that appeared twice.[11] And he took sole credit for the visual effects on the same film—thereby winning his only Oscar—despite the bulk of the work being done by Douglas Trumbull, Wally Veevers, Con Pederson, and Tom Howard.

If you have never read anything (until now) about the remarkably tasteless bit of artistic self-aggrandizement that opens *2001*, it can only be because, as I say, anyone who writes about Kubrick is already down with the idea of Kubrick being second only to God in the realm of creativity. My guess is that people who love Kubrick love the idea that self-aggrandizement can pass for art. I think they love the idea of the superior man creating superior works and being revered for it, as if this was what "art" were all about. Once upon a time, I loved that idea too. I just didn't—couldn't—love Kubrick, the filmmaker who most fully embodies the cult of the visionary artistic genius.

That anomaly was the splinter in my brain that eventually led to this book.

The man

> "Everyone pretty much acknowledges he's the man. I still feel that underrates him."
>
> —Jack Nicholson, on Kubrick

No one who cares about movies can be entirely indifferent to Stanley Kubrick (even if they are indifferent to his films). On AMC's "Greatest Directors of All Time" list, Kubrick is ranked at no. 2, just behind Alfred Hitchcock and just before Billy Wilder.[12] In Ranker's "The Greatest Directors in Movie History," Kubrick is ranked in the top position, before Hitch (Scorsese is in third position).[13] On the British Film Institute's list of 50 greatest movies, *2001: A Space Odyssey* is ranked in sixth position. In a separate poll by the BFI, for which 358 filmmakers chose their favorite films, the film comes in second place (after *Vertigo*).

Kubrick is both the critics' darling and the filmmaker's most cherished vision of himself (not herself[14]). Yet, unlike perhaps the only other English-language filmmaker with equal status—Hitchcock, also born under the sign of Leo—Kubrick's status is disproportionate to his popularity with ordinary moviegoing audiences. Hitchcock was a popular entertainer long before he was raised up to the throne of film genius. Kubrick had to first be raised up by critics (and other filmmakers) in order to become "popular." Juxtaposing Kubrick with Hitchcock may be useful in other ways. Hitchcock was a filmmaker whose art was directed almost exclusively toward pleasing his audience. He measured his success as a filmmaker in terms of how well audiences received his films, to the extent that he considered *Vertigo* a failure because of its poor box office receipts. Kubrick, on the other hand, seemed to go out of his way to confound audience expectations—or at least (a key point), this is how he has come to be *seen* by those who revere his work.

Hitchcock prided himself on his ability to manipulate his audience, to play them like an organ, as he put it, meaning to invoke in them whatever strong emotions he wanted them to feel. Hitchcock is known as the master of suspense because of his ability to emotionally hook viewers and pull them along, giving them the sort of experience they expected from a Hitchcock movie. A Kubrick movie offers the opposite kind of experience: detached, abstract, emotionally uninvolving, but fascinating precisely *because* of its strangeness and unfamiliarity, its apparent refusal to hit the standard emotional and visceral cues that filmgoers require from movies. Hitchcock *catered* to audiences, but Kubrick aimed to confound them; in the process, I think, he flattered them (a certain kind of viewer) into feeling included in a hermetic and heady experience of "higher" moviegoing. While Hitchcock prided himself on being a superb entertainer (his motto was "It's only a movie"), Kubrick prided himself on offering something more than mere entertainment.

Hitchcock made 57 movies in a 45-year career. Kubrick made 13 over a period of 46 years. Of those 13, only 5 (*Paths of Glory, Spartacus, Dr. Strangelove, 2001: A Space Odyssey*, and *A Clockwork Orange*) were "popular" with audiences at the time of their release. *The Killing* was a small hit, but the rest of his films were seen as disappointments—both critically and commercially—on their initial release. Yet Kubrick's reputation has not only continued to build over the years—including and perhaps especially after his death—it has by now attained an almost saintly aura, one that surpasses Hitchcock's and probably that of every other filmmaker who ever lived. For some, it is not enough to praise Kubrick as a great filmmaker. It may not even be enough to assert that he is the *greatest* filmmaker of all time. Somehow, he must be placed in a class all his own, a class to which no other filmmaker belongs. Unlike other filmmakers, no matter how brilliant (so say his devotees), Kubrick *was not making ordinary movies*.

The idea that Kubrick was making movies that were out of the ordinary is one that began as a purely aesthetic proposition, namely, that Kubrick's movies were more technically accomplished, intellectually profound, and aesthetically innovative than other movies. Yet, over time, and since his death, it has evolved, or mutated, into something both more literal and dogmatic and, at the same time, more abstract and bizarre. There is now an entire subculture of Kubrick admirers and exegetists who are analyzing Kubrick's movies, not with the usual tools of film criticism nor with the aim of praising the films' cinematic brilliance (though this is always inherent in their evaluations), but in the belief that they provide coded, secret information about—*everything*, from the Moon landing to the hidden nature of reality itself.

How this happened, and why—and the extent to which it was the result of *Kubrick's conscious intention*—is what this book is about.

Deny all knowledge

> "But what chess teaches you is that you must sit there calmly and think about whether it's really a good idea and whether there are other, better ideas."
>
> —Stanley Kubrick

Before getting to the many examples of "the Kubrick code," it's worth mentioning how this subculture of Kubraphilia has become large and vocal enough to enter the mainstream. The main ambassador for the dedicated marginals has been Rodney Ascher's fascinating 2012 documentary, *Room 237*. Ascher's film showcases "a group of obsessed Kubrick loyalists to carefully examine, frame by frame, some of the hidden messages behind his controversial 1980 film *The Shining*."[15] Broken down into nine segments, each chapter focuses on a specific element of Kubrick's film that "may reveal hidden clues and hint at a bigger thematic oeuvre."[16] The clues range from background Native American art, oblique references to Nazi Germany, almost impossible-to-read references to incest on the cover of a *Playgirl* magazine, to apparent continuity errors, specific camera movements, long dissolves, creating subliminal illusions via subtle image juxtaposition, and mapping out the exact layout of the hotel and carefully dissecting the tricycle route that Danny takes. While all the interpretations are distinct, even mutually exclusive, what they have in common is the belief that Kubrick used *a vast array of methods and subterfuges to subtly manipulate his audience*. To varying degrees, all of the readings are persuasive, which is what makes *Room 237* such a fascinating, even mind-bending, experience—in some ways, much more than *The Shining* (though it also makes Kubrick's film more intriguing).

Ascher's film had some trouble with fair usage of all the Kubrick footage, but eventually it found widespread distribution and became popular enough to catch the attention of Kubrick's own nearest and dearest. Predictably enough, they were having none of it. Leon Vitali, who first worked with Kubrick as an actor in *Barry Lyndon* and went on to become the director's assistant, called the majority of *Room 237* "pure gibberish." Allegedly (he says), he was "falling about laughing most of the time" and that "there are ideas espoused in the movie that I know to be total balderdash."[17]

> Vitali, though, is eager to set the record straight. What about Jack Nicholson's recitation of "Three Little Pigs" as one of the many ties of the film's apparent nods to the Holocaust? Vitali says the detail was an improv, and that Kubrick called up the mother of child actor Danny Lloyd (who plays Danny Torrance) for suggestions for "a few lines for Jack that would make him sound threatening and nasty," and that "she had the words to 'Three Little Pigs' right there." Danny's sweater showing the Apollo 11 rocket? "It was just the sort of thing that a kid that age would have liked," Vitali told the *New York Times*.[18]

This last is a reference to Jay Weidner's theory that *The Shining* is Kubrick's coded confession to filming the fake Moon landing footage. Needless to say, Vitali's non-denial denial falls short of bringing this sort of imaginative theorizing down to Earth. Considerably more emphatic in her denials was Kubrick's youngest daughter, Vivian, who wrote "an open letter vehemently chiding those who believe it to be true."[19] A Tweet by Vivian Kubrick from July 5, 2016, received 192 replies, 1,419 retweets, and 2,192 likes and was titled "Re: Faked Moon Landings. Many people have asked me about this. And this feels like the right time to respond …" There was a longer piece by Vivian attached as an image:

> Surely (?!) an artist, such as my father, whose profound degree of artistic integrity is self-evident, whose political/social conscious-ness is manifestly present in nearly every film he made. Whose highly controversial subject matter literally put his life at risk, and

yet he continued to make the film's [sic] he made ... don't you think he'd be the very last person EVER to assist the US Government in such a terrible betrayal of its people?!?

There are many, very real conspiracies that have happened throughout our history, are happening presently, I'm only too aware of the dreadful manipulations perpetrated by governments, secret services, banksters, the military-industrial-complex etc. But, claims that the moon landings were faked and filmed by my father? I just can't understand it!!? How can anyone believe that one of the greatest defenders of mankind would commit such an act of betrayal?

My father's artistic works are his unimpeachable defence!

Finally, my love for my father notwithstanding, I actually knew him! I lived and worked with him, so forgive my harshness when I state categorically: the so called "truth" these malicious cranks persist in forwarding—that my father conspired with the US Government to "fake the moon landings"—is manifestly A GROTESQUE LIE.[20]

This denial was seen by mainstream media pundits as definitive. Yet definition is in the eye of the beholder, and Vivian Kubrick's denial did little, probably nothing, to check the progress of this lively meme. If anything, it may have only fanned the flames. Though Kubrick's daughter is herself something of a "conspiracy theorist" (an ex-Scientologist, she appeared on arch conspiracist Alex Jones' *InfoWars* program), apparently she has little awareness of the intricacy of the belief that has developed around her father—or of the depth of deception which it already presupposes. Clearly, for those who believe the Moon landing was faked by Kubrick, it is a very small leap of imagination to think that his daughter was either kept in the dark about it (like the rest of us) or that she is one more agent of deception. Simply put, Vivian Kubrick's denial-cum-accusation did little to define anything besides her own position on the matter.

By dismissing the theory that her father faked the Moon landing as a "GROTESQUE LIE," Vivian seriously underestimated the power of human belief. It is not a lie but a *myth* that has formed around Kubrick and one that, as I will demonstrate, he partially created. It is also one that now has a life of its own.

This is very much the point of *The Kubrickon*.

Immersion criticism

> "Self-deception ... might therefore profitably be construed simply as the opposite of exploration in the face of anomaly ... This failure leads to a mental state in which the self-deceiver continues to hold beliefs that have been indicated as problematic by his or her own affective response ... The greater the perceived anomaly—that is, the broader or more basic the plans, goals, or conceptions it disrupts—the more negative the affective response, and the more potent the motivation for self-deception."
> —Jordan Peterson, Erin Driver-Linn, and Colin DeYoung, "Self-Deception and Impaired Categorization of Anomaly"

Next up, we have "immersion criticism," something that

> can't really be done unless you watch a movie 10 or 100 or 1,000 times. It's based on the belief that symbolic, ancillary details inside a film are infinitely more important than the surface dialogue or the superficial narrative. And it's not just a matter of noticing things other people miss, because that can be done by anyone who's perceptive; it's a matter of noticing things that the director included to indicate his true, undisclosed intention. In other words, it's not an interpretive reading—it's an inflexible, clandestine reality that matters way more than anything else. And it's usually insane. Now, there's a reason all these examples come from Kubrick films: *Immersion Criticism only works if you believe the director really did have some type of secret objective.*[21]

The astute reader may notice at once that this last point is a case of circular reasoning. It also follows that the more one practices immersive criticism and discovers what one thinks are intentional but hidden details encoded in a work of art, the more one will come to believe (will *have* to believe) that the creator had "some type of secret objective." That said, it's probably fair to say that this circle does *begin* with the belief that an artist is somehow more than just an artist or that he or she has some objective that transcends (what we think of as) the run-of-the-mill objectives of art. This is something I believe *is* true of Kubrick, i.e., that he set this particular ball in motion, a ball that was rolling so long and gathered such momentum that eventually it was bound to wind up bouncing around the ears of his nearest and dearest, causing all manner of consternation.

John Fell Ryan is one of the immersive critics of *Room 237* who had the inspired notion of playing *The Shining* forward and backward at the same time, and superimposing the two together. Refreshingly self-aware and self-effacing, Ryan writes how

> A detail in *The Shining* tugs at your brain a little, piques your curiosity. You spend some time with a digital copy of film taking screenshots. Next thing you know, you've been up for days counting lightbulbs and balloons, feverishly cataloging placement of different water-coolers, looking for deep numerological significance in every time-code stamp.

Some of the examples he discovered (besides that cover of *Playgirl* magazine):

> As Wendy takes a tour of the kitchen on her first day at the Overlook she passes by three clocks. The first is above the elevator as she passes through the fire exit, and reads 1:30. The second clock is on the kitchen wall as she passes from the freezer to the store room, and reads 12:50, 40 minutes earlier. The third clock is in the green service hallway and reads 10:55, one hour and 55 minutes earlier. So over the course of under four minutes screen time, the clocks reverse a total of two hours and 35 minutes.[22]

Examples of supposedly intentional weirdness in *The Shining* are often trivial, but endearingly so, such as how there is no toilet paper in room 237 (the horror!). Or the way Wendy's knife in the final scenes keeps switching from one hand to the other and back again. Needless to say, such oversights and continuity errors in the work of other filmmakers would either go unnoticed or be ignored as evidence of an overworked director or an editor snoozing at his Moviola. Nor would they—even in the hundreds—be likely to give a filmmaker a reputation for being a gnomic genius intent on confounding viewers with inexplicable anomalies and inside jokes planted throughout his movies. It is the *combination* of Kubrick's famously exacting eye for detail, and his seemingly inexhaustible insistence on accuracy and precision, with these sorts of "errors" that has led to Kubrick's unique reputation in this regard.

Even so, this idea might never have gained traction were it not for the fact that Kubrick apparently *did* have a tendency for embedding super-subtle clues within the texture of his movies, clues that *could* be taken for errors, but almost certainly weren't. Most famously, there is the murderous super-computer in *2001: A Space Odyssey*, "officially" (according to Arthur C. Clarke) named HAL as an abbreviation of Heuristically programmed ALgorithmic computer. After the film was released, some commentators noticed the three letters H-A-L come one letter before the letters I-B-M. That this was a deliberate dig at the leading computer company at that time was denied by both Clarke and Kubrick. Clarke even went so far as to claim they "would have changed the name had [they] spotted the coincidence," because they were in quite good standing with IBM, and IBM would not wish to have their name associated with a murderously malfunctioning super-computer.

The reader can decide how likely Kubrick and Clarke's denials are, but whatever the case it made little or no difference unless it was to keep the rumors alive. At this point, I'd wager that more people are aware of the HAL–IBM "coincidence" than they are of the phrase "heuristically programmed algorithmic" (of which, let's admit, "HAL" seems a less than obvious choice for a derivative).

If this is—arguably—the first recorded case of coded information embedded in a Kubrick film, then possibly the first example of an important clue being concealed in a bit of seemingly trivial screen action is also found in the same film. In the middle section of *2001*, the part which is the closest to a conventional narrative, HAL begins to malfunction and eventually kills all the crew except for one, Dave, who disconnects HAL (after which he meets the Monolith and becomes God/ the star child, on its way to Earth). In the lead-in to HAL's "malfunction," there is a seemingly unimportant scene in which one of the crew, Poole, plays chess with HAL and HAL tells Poole, "I'm sorry Frank, I think you missed it." HAL lays out a brief series of moves that "he" can now make, leading to Poole's defeat. Poole accepts HAL's forecast and resigns. Kubrick was well-known to be a very serious chess player, and, not surprisingly, the game between HAL and Poole in this scene was based on a real-life game. But HAL *misrepresents the situation* to Poole, making it seem worse than it is, thereby ensuring Poole's resignation.

There's some debate about the exact meaning of the scene. Is HAL lying and finding out he can get away with it? Is he testing to see if Poole is paying attention? Or is he starting to malfunction? Whatever the case (I am not a chess player), what seemed at first like a trivial scene has since been identified (rightly or wrongly) as a significant turning point in the storyline, namely, the first moment when HAL is seen to act unreliably. Kubrick would have known that no viewer—at least on first viewing—could have spotted this. Yet he chose to embed a significant clue to his story in the minutiae of a scene, in something as seemingly irrelevant as the pieces on a chess board. Leaving aside the symbolic content of the scene, one obvious result of this is that, when more diligent viewers found such a vital clue, they would be immediately alerted that Kubrick films *not only invite but demand a rigorous and relentless combing for clues and coded information.*

The game was afoot.

Extraordinary facts and ridiculous flights of hermeneutic fantasy

> "The military-industrial complex has become the military-entertainment complex. The entertainment industry is both a major source of innovative ideas and technology, and the training ground for what might be called posthuman warfare."
> —Timothy Lenoir, "Technology and Biotechnology: Fashioning the Military-Entertainment Complex"

The spectrum of supposedly concealed Kubrick code in the filmmaker's oeuvre ranges from the sublime to the ridiculous—if not the grotesque. Yet through it all, which end of the spectrum we find ourselves on remains highly subjective—which is very much the point. An intriguing blog article from 2015, entitled "Deep Blue Dreams: 666 Days of Stanley Kubrick," begins with this: "Stanley Kubrick Died 666 Days Before January 1st, 2001." After pointing this out, the writer adds: "the day on which [Kubrick] died—March 7th—also happened to be the 66th day of the year!" He then claims that the number of the beast:

> is all over Kubrick's films. In *A Clockwork Orange*, when Alex de Large has been reintroduced to his two old droogies Georgie & Dim, only to find that they have become police officers, their badges are visible, & we see that one of them is #665 & the other is #667, implying that Alex is the missing #666. Or take the space-ship Discovery from *2001: A Space Odyssey*, as seen from the rear: The ship's engines are ensconced in three separate hexagons, or six-sided figures. There it is, 666, the number of Kubrick's magickal son/sun, right there, smack on the ass of Kubrick's cosmic spermatozoa, staring

CHILDREN OF KUBRICK   15

> you right in the face as it drifts out to fertilize the Egg of Space & conceive the New Man. Kubrick is virtually taunting the viewer with this arrangement throughout all of his films, just daring you to see it, & laughing as you miss it completely.[23] The fact that Kubrick died 666 days before the actual year 2001 just seems like icing on the cake, one final sneer from beyond the grave of the Master Magician who relished the notion that nobody ever really understood him, or his work. Something akin to a cosmic giggle. End of story. Or is it?[24]

Undaunted by his Master's mockery, the author goes on to wonder, reasonably enough, "what happened 666 days *before* Stanley Kubrick's death?" He starts with 7 March 1999, and counts backward to 666, landing on May 11, 1997. What happened that day? The computer known as "Deep Blue" defeated chess champion Gary Kasparov in "Game 6."

> This was the first time an Artificial Intelligence was able to defeat a Human Intelligence in a professional-style chess match. It made headlines the world over ... Entire books have been written on the subject of just this Machine, just this match. One of them is called "HAL's Legacy: *2001's* Computer as Dream & Reality." There is a chapter in this book which compares the play-styles of HAL & Deep Blue ... but in my cursory research it appears to me that nobody has pointed out the insanely obvious fact that Deep Blue *looks exactly like the Monolith*, & by extension HAL itself. There's not even a little tidbit somewhere (that I can find) noting that "Deep Blue's design was inspired by the film *2001.*" Nothing, just the picture. Oh, & a one-sentence comment on chess.com from 7 years ago, noting the similarity in appearance. Note also the prominent IBM logo on the upper face of Deep Blue, & the well-known fact that HAL is a cypher for IBM, a company which features prominently throughout *2001: A Space Odyssey* & which it is very strongly implied were the original builders of the HAL 9000. Clarke & Kubrick chalked this up to coincidence, but come on, yeah right.

Reminding us that this happened "exactly 666 days before Stanley Kubrick's death, which itself occurred 666 days before January 1st, 2001," the author asks "how can this be? Extraordinary claims may require extraordinary evidence, but what of extraordinary facts? What do they require?"

To many, such as Alex Sayf Cummings (the author of a 2017 article, "*Eyes Wide Shut* and The Paranoid Style in American Pop Culture"), such facts are only extraordinary when placed in the context of "ridiculous flights of hermeneutic fantasy" (hermeneutic is a fancy word for interpretive).

> What makes this all possible is the legend of Kubrick as the perfectionist. (The word "perfectionism" comes up frequently in Wikipedia entries on the filmmaker and his work.) He has the reputation of a director for whom every granular detail on screen is purposeful and rich with intent—a director who is also a consummate cinematographer, art director, and general freebase control freak. Thus, the box of Calumet baking powder in *The Shining* is not just an aesthetic detail or, God forbid, a random throwaway gesture, but the opening into a rich and complex tapestry of meanings about European conquest of the Americas and the return of the repressed. Given the license to view every pixel as a potential message in a bottle, the Kubrick interpreter can make the text mean almost anything, because that's what Stanley intended. It is perhaps well to ask what this exegetic excess says about Kubrick and the generation that grew up with his movies.[25]

Establishment critic Armond White was even more scathing—also obtuse—when he reviewed *Room 237*. He referred to the film as a "disturbing vision of post-cinephilia asininity" that demonstrated "a current style of cinematic illiteracy that has replaced critical thinking."

> Actually an embarrassment to the intellectually ambitious Kubrick, *Room 237* shows that the Kubrick cult consists of that breed who like [sic] to think they think. However, the hypotheses presented (and seemingly validated by use of actual—pirated?—Kubrick clips) resist rationality. I've long realized that Kubrick's stature among film buffs certified a paradigm shift from the Hitchcock era when the legendary master of suspense—and of montage—inspired a different, popular enthusiasm than Kubrick whose esoteric, post-WWII misanthropy fed recent generations of kiddie nihilists who, considering themselves especially smart, responded to his stiff (non-sensual, thus anti-Hitchcockian) compositions. (They're now the Fincher/Nolan kids.)

White went on to lament the "weird ecstasies of obsessive overthinking" and "contemporary film criticism shallowness" of the new Kubrick cultists, and referred to "the fantasies produced by uneducated responses to the Kubrick myth and the irrationality of *The Shining*" as "hero-worship, not analysis."

> Reverence for Stanley Kubrick overwhelms any understanding of *The Shining*. It is symptomatic of today's celebrity veneration—the flip-side of the feeling of nothingness that makes nerds bow down to the likes of Nolan, Fincher, Paul Thomas Anderson, Soderbergh and Kubrick. So they fantasize about *The Shining*'s supposed profundity ... The Kubrick cult dispenses with traditional humanist notions of art appreciation ... Without any schooling in visual or literary interpretation, the Kubrick cult is left to bizarre fantasizing ... When Ascher isn't holding Kubrick obsessives up to ridicule, his presentation yet implies the same credibility the Internet gives fanboy bloggers. Like Internet criticism, *Room 237* resembles the kind of conspiracy theory mania that kooks used to put on single-spaced mimeographed sheets and pass out on street corners.

White ends his excoriation with a melodramatic flourish that betrays his own allegiance: "*Room 237* is another confirmation of the end of cinephilia."[26] But his criticism not only badly misses the boat (there is nothing remotely ridiculing about Ascher's treatment of Kubrick obsessives), it also appears oddly contradictory in lamenting "the end of cinephilia" while blaming it on Kubrick obsessives, who surely come under the rubric of cinephiles, however unorthodox? Yet, at the same time, I can't help but sympathize with White's (and Cummings') exasperation, because there *is* something depressing about the hermeneutics of the Kubraphiles—even if I would extend it to those (like Cummings) who only praise Kubrick as a masterful cultural commentator and react territorially when less conventional (and more conspiratorial) cinephiles try to claim Dr. Stanley as their own.

Clearly, there is a gulf, and bridging it may itself require some *apparent* flights of fantasy, if only to imagine a way that both sides of this great divide might not only be wrong, but also, in some mysterious fashion, right. To bridge that gulf requires a closer look at what the purportedly more "grounded" faction insists on seeing—and dismissing—as Conspiracy Kooksville.

7. WHAT IF KUBRICK APPROACHED HIS MOVIES AS EXPRESSIONS OF CONSCIOUS INTENT, NOT UNCONSCIOUS CONTENT? — NOT AS AN ARTIST BUT AS A (MAD) SCIENTIST??

(2001?)

8. HE COULD THEN DESIGN MOVIES IN SUCH A WAY AS TO PERFECTLY RESEMBLE ART YET BE EMPTY OF UNCONSCIOUS MEANING

9. BUT WHAT WOULD BE THE END GOAL?

IF ART = EXPRESSION, THEN SCIENCE = DISCOVER OR INVENTION.

SO WHAT WAS THE SCIENTIFIC BREAKTHROUGH THAT KUBRICK WAS TRYING TO ACHIEVE??

10. GREAT STANLEY! I THINK I'VE GOT IT!!!

CHAPTER 2

Full metal emperor

> "Kubrick himself, and the film version of *The Shining*, in particular, is the locus of a certain kind of obsessive yet strangely inarticulate worship; the faithful tend to incant the words 'genius' and 'masterpiece' and 'great' over and over again, as if those terms constituted the workings of an argument rather than its conclusion. These are people in thrall to the very idea of greatness, and they cleave ferociously to their idol."
>
> —Laura Miller, Salon.com

A prisoner finds scratchings on his prison wall, made by a former inmate. The scratchings appear to show the inner workings of the prison and—since they were done from inside the cell—can only be the result of a failed escape attempt. Instead of trying to find out if the diagrams are accurate and attempting his own escape, the inmate deems the scratchings "art" and forms a cult around their maker.

There is a particular sort of intellectual enrapturement that Kubrick films tend to invoke in people, one that seems to go along with *a susceptibility to being possessed*—or programmed—by outside influences.

On the one hand, Stanley Kubrick fans seem to be lacking in imagination when they are in the presence of their Master. On the other hand, the many exegetists of *The Shining* display a *rich* imagination in the ways they "decode" the film's supposedly hidden meanings. Would they be willing to allow the possibility that their findings were the fruit of their own imagination? I suspect not. It's as if Kubrick's films "hijack" the viewers' imaginations and redirect them *to Kubrick himself*: he gets all the credit, and the exegetists get to feel like Charlie Manson with the White Album—or Renfield in *Dracula*—picking up messages from the Master rather than from their own unconscious.

Some of the refutations I have heard from "the field" (that of Kubraphiles for whom "a mountain is a mountain") are more emotional/ideological than rational. The idea that Kubrick's films might not be the irrefutable masterpieces they have been taken for, but something different (though not necessarily something *less*), is *ipso facto* unacceptable. Anyone with any sense of "good cinema" knows that Kubrick was a genius. Even—or especially—other filmmakers agree. Such arguments create their own "proofs"; taking something eminently questionable as a basis, they launch themselves off this flimsy foundation—like fake Moon landings.

There is something about the sort of influence that causes awe and admiration that has a tendency to *stupefy* us. To stupefy means to render incapable of thinking or feeling properly, but also to astonish, shock, or take our breath away. This may be why those who do resist Kubrick's spell—Pauline Kael being an outstanding example—do so with a kind of stubborn rejection of even his better qualities. It isn't really possible to be lukewarm about films like *A Clockwork Orange* or *Eyes Wide Shut*. I feel I have to actively *dislike* these movies, even to loathe them, in order to counteract the pressure they exert—as cultural artifacts—to be viewed as masterpieces.

One purpose of the present work is to examine our assumptions about what constitutes art, and whether it can ever be separated from what we think of as propaganda, or perception management. My primary thesis about Kubrick is inseparable from a lifelong issue with those who admire his work—namely, that they have taken the finger for the Moon, the clothes for the emperor, and been lured into the locus of a certain kind of obsessive yet strangely inarticulate worship.

Needful guesswork

"Like any artist a part of what I want is to make my needful guesswork, my cherished misapprehensions, so persuasive and glorious that they become more valuable than any fact could ever be."
—Jonathan Lethem, *Fear of Music*

In the *Fargo* TV show (created by self-confessed Kubrick-apostle Noah Hawley), in the penultimate episode of the third season, Emmitt (Ewan McGregor) asks: "A lie is not a lie if you believe it's true—do you think that?"

If we are honest, the answer to Emmitt's question is that we *have* to think that. What other choice do we have? The alternative is to be forced to admit that we rarely, if ever, know when we are lying or not. For how many times in our lives do we believe things that are not true and act accordingly?

So then, how can we distinguish between a lie, an honest mistake, a fabrication of truth, a delusion, and the artist's "needful guesswork"? And can truly meaningful discovery about *anything* happen without the latter, without a speculative hypothesis, imaginative interpretation of evidence, and wild propositions? How is an artist to know when their guesswork is delusional, when it is wishful thinking (unconscious lies) or self-serving misapprehensions, and when it is inspired and audacious insight, just waiting around to be confirmed by slower, duller minds?

The answer is: we can't, not until later at least. And even then, we may not be sure. Is being embraced by consensus and inducted into the halls of fame reserved for stone-cold facts really proof that we are right? Or is it only evidence that our guesses were appealing enough to the majority—useful for propping up its cherished delusions—for it to bestow upon us the "Snopes" seal of agreement? Is the reverential chorus of "Yes, you are right!" proof we have nailed reality, or only that we have sold out to an established lie?

Is this work fiction or nonfiction? The answer is both and neither. It is a work of needful guesswork, applied to agreed-upon facts. Facts such as Stanley Kubrick is a man who was born and who died, who made a series of movies that were appraised (and revered) by others (critics and filmmakers especially), and that have now become an intrinsic part of our culture. That he had certain connections and relationships—some known, some not—that informed his work and career, both visibly and invisibly. His aims, objectives, values, and motivations are and always will be unknown, and while they can be guessed at I would say it is needless: we don't have to know the cook's innermost nature to work out the ingredients of the meal.

The Kubrickon begins with a premise and works its way backward from that premise in an attempt to demonstrate it. This may seem like poor science but, from another perspective, it is the essence of science. Logic demands that if we have already decided what our conclusion is we are going to cherry-pick those facts that support it, and ignore, dismiss, be blind, deaf, and dumb to those that don't. Poor science, then, but necessary art? For the unifying vision of any written work belongs to its author, and if I hadn't already come up with a necessary guess to explain the evidence of my *experience* of Stanley Kubrick's oeuvre and career (namely, that it is *uncommonly and inexplicably overrated*), I would never have written this work at all.

All this began as an attempt to demonstrate both how and why Kubrick films are nowhere near as good as people keep claiming they are. More precisely (i.e., less subjectively), to explore the gulf between my subjective experience of Kubrick films and the consensus view of them that exists, out there, at large, in the world. What is the nature, substance, and meaning of this gulf? Why does it exist, how did it come to be, and by what means can it be bridged, or perhaps closed forever?

Fiction writing is a stacked deck and a loaded dice. All fiction aspires to become nonfiction, in the mind of the reader at least, and for as long as it takes to be read. And where else is such a transformation to occur if not in the mind of the reader? For without the reader, this forest is empty.

The same is (roughly or exactly) true of a scientific or philosophical hypothesis (or, for that matter, a political or religious one): the aim is to persuade others of its veracity, to make the grade and undergo a slow, steady and seamless transition from fiction to nonfiction, subjective to objective reality. When legend becomes fact, print the legend. For this to happen, the author, first of all, has to suspend disbelief long enough and well enough to forget having done so, and keep it up for at least as long as it takes to write his nonfiction narrative, or novelistic essay, and unleash it.

A fiction author may not (some would say must not) know how his characters will end up or quite who they are at the start. But he, she, we, or I must *desire* for them to become as real as they can become. We also know this points to a spectrum: some fictions are less real than others, and not all characters are created equal. This is a fact, and facts—in a post-truth world—are becoming more and more awkward, unwieldy, and inconvenient, hence more and more dramatically interesting. Fiction, on the other hand, is becoming increasingly self-serving, sentimental (even when nihilistic), and palpably delusional—unreal—and hence less and less dramatically relevant. The psychological operation of culture has made mockingbirds of us all.

What coheres and compels must be (at least in my needful guesswork) what most closely resembles truth. The hypothesis must fit the data, just as the data must support the hypothesis. Character and story are one continuum; evidence and argument are the same. The evidence must argue for itself, but also, far less objectively and more elusively, the argument must cohere to the point of *itself becoming evidence*, the recreation of a crime scene in lieu of a body.

Cultural warfare

> "The only thing we can learn from history is the fact that you can't learn anything from history."
> —Stanley Kubrick

I propose that Kubrick's later films are cultural artifacts *designed as scientific instruments to interact with human consciousness and cross-bond with it* (create obsession), *as a means of gathering data from the species and importing it to a machine database.*

This experiment only became fully possible with the development of the internet, which, perhaps not coincidentally, began in the late 1960s, during the time Kubrick was involved with *2001* and (so I will argue) with covert scientific government programs.

Stanley Kubrick's last few movies do not work dramatically for a number of reasons. The principle one is that Kubrick was only using dramatic cinematic structure as a vehicle, or outer form (a Trojan Horse), to contain *scientific memeplexes* and inject them into the culture. Kubrick's aim was to make his movies *appear* like movies *just enough* to get past the average viewer's psychic defenses and make them *believe* they had seen a more or less ordinary movie, even if a strangely incoherent and unaffecting one—that being Kubrick's famous "style"—and one that initially caused *a general feeling of disappointment*.

(According to Kubrick biographer John Baxter, Kubrick believed that films "depended on a small group of 'non-submersible' sequences—five or six scenes which supported the whole argument of the film. Once these were constructed and anchored in place, the gaps between them could be disguised with brief narrative links, or a voice-over". p. 159).

Let us suppose that the Kubrick obsessives filing through every frame of his movies with a fine tooth comb are right. Let us suppose that the reason there is no coherent narrative (only the semblance of one) in

Kubrick's movies is that they are artifacts that attempt to *imitate the structure of the universe*. Let's imagine they are designed mathematically, according to ancient principles that recognize the equivalency of all the major scientific disciplines, the correspondences between the musical scale, the color spectrum, geometry, planetary arrangements, and so forth. Edgar Allan Poe attempted to write poetry according to mathematical principles (his most famous example is "The Raven"), so why not Kubrick?

The question then becomes, not why not, but *why*?

My final proposition is the most unlikely yet. What if Kubrick's aim was not to lead his viewers into a deeper understanding of the universe but to infect them with his own dis-ease, namely, the obsessive desire to map and replicate existence? What if his plan was to transform his fans, the dedicated viewers, into *unwitting participants in an elaborate, carefully orchestrated, long-term experiment*?

TL;DR: Kubrick's movies are designed to lure rats into a laboratory-constructed maze, there to observe them and, eventually, train them and put them to work.

* * *

> "Art is almost always a part of someone's ongoing war with reality. Infiltrating the subconscious is the goal of any and every screenwriter with skill, and not by any means exclusive to some meme-cult. By watching a movie, or a TV series, you are signing up to be enlisted in another man's psycho-spiritual war. In the brutal artillery barrage of images and emotions, they are re-sculpting the landscape of consensus reality to conform to the terrain of their own selfish dreams."
>
> —Schwab, "Lucid Dreaming"

As far as I know (not having worked it out in advance, since this is not an academic work), there are two primary theses to this work. The first is somewhat fantastical, largely speculative, and possibly unprovable. It is, bluntly put, that Stanley Kubrick was involved in a secret project to create artificial intelligence via a stimulating and harvesting of collective human attention, using a combination of his film opus and the internet to do so. The second hypothesis (or hyper-thesis) is that Kubrick's career was shaped, directed, and enabled as part of an ongoing government, military, scientific, and intelligence program of social-cultural engineering, popularly known within the conspiratainment circles as "a psy-op" (a psychological operation).

This latter may sound improbable to some, especially to cinephiles who admire Kubrick and regard artistic creators as a special and even sacrosanct breed of independent thinkers who emerge spontaneously from and through a given culture and transform it through their own efforts.

To those who have studied deep politics and espionage, such an idea will seem quite depressingly mundane. *Who Paid the Piper? The CIA and the Cultural Cold War* (retitled *The Cultural Cold War: The CIA and the World of Arts and Letters* in the US) by Frances Stonor Saunders, for example, recounts how the Central Intelligence Agency played an active role in the infiltration, co-opting, and in some cases the wholecloth creation, of artistic movements in the mid-20th century, ostensibly to counteract Communism and expand American political influence. Much of the CIA's funding went through the Congress for Cultural Freedom; as Saunders writes, "Whether they liked it or not, whether they knew it or not, there were few writers, poets, artists, historians, scientists, or critics in postwar Europe whose names were not in some way linked to this covert enterprise" (p. 2).

Alternatively, one doesn't have to dig any deeper than the work of Carl Bernstein (the famous *Washington Post* reporter played by Dustin Hoffman in *All the President's Men*) to learn about Operation Mockingbird, a large-scale program of the CIA that began in the early 1950s. Mockingbird's goal was to infiltrate domestic news media for propaganda purposes, and this it did with predictable efficacy and thoroughness. Its range of fronts spanned from student organizations and newsletters to leading national newspapers and magazines in the US. Phil Graham from the *Washington Post* ran the project within the press, and according to a 1979 biography of *Post* owner Katharine Graham (*Katharine the Great*, by Deborah Davis), "By the early 1950s, [CIA co-founder] Wisner 'owned' respected members of the *New York Times*, *Newsweek*, *CBS* and other communications vehicles."[27] (Graham was played by Meryl Streep in the 2017 Spielberg movie *The Post*; in the post-truth age, the reputation of US news media is in need of some high-level spin doctoring.)

In 1951, CIA director Allen Dulles persuaded Cord Meyer to join the CIA, and Meyer became Mockingbird's "principal operative."[28]

After 1953, the media network was overseen by Dulles, by which time (as Bernstein reports) Operation Mockingbird had major influence over 25 US newspapers and wire agencies.[29] The specific networks were run by people with well-known liberal but pro-American big business and anti-Soviet views, such as William S. Paley (CBS), Henry Luce (*Time* and *Life*), Arthur Hays Sulzberger (the *New York Times*), Alfred Friendly (managing editor of the *Washington Post*), Jerry O'Leary (the *Washington Star*), Hal Hendrix (*Miami News*), Barry Bingham, Sr. (*Louisville Courier-Journal*), James S. Copley (*Copley News Services*), and Joseph Harrison (the *Christian Science Monitor*).

I have written about the subject of social and cultural engineering much more extensively in *Prisoner of Infinity*, *The Vice of Kings*, and *16 Maps of Hell*; the above is only meant to give some minimal context for understanding the other primary thesis of *The Kubrickon*: that culture, as most people understand the term—which technically is called "mass culture," meaning the mass-produced and mass mediated forms of consumer culture—is and always has been the product of a myriad of intersecting, semi-covert, and wholly *intentional* agendas on the part of a hidden ruling class (of unknown uniformity) by which to manipulate the public into modes of worship, belief, and behavior. What the CIA's hands-on cultural investments, as outlined above, indicate, I believe, is only the tip of an iceberg that, if uncovered, would be seen to incorporate mass culture in its entirety. *No successful artist—which is to say leading cultural figure with the corresponding social influence—becomes so without the support, covert or otherwise, of this invisible apparatus.*

We are wise to consider this when looking at a creative individual with the sort of cultural, historical influence as Stanley Kubrick.

Yet, more than using the strange case of Stanley Kubrick to demonstrate the thesis of cultural engineering, I wish to use the thesis of cultural engineering as a means to reevaluate Kubrick and his work and see if that reevaluation holds up to, and even trumps, the reigning evaluation—that of an independent artistic genius who came out of nowhere and made his way to the top of the cultural pyramid through a mix of sheer talent, perseverance, and crazy good luck.

I am aware—how could I not be?—that this is like the child pointing at the emperor and saying he is naked. It is an apparent disservice to the dignity of royalty. But it's my belief that in fact the real disservice is done to the emperor—or the alleged cinematic genius—by believing in the illusion he has managed to create, since, as a result, no one will ever suspect just how cold the emperor's bollocks might be.

This is the problem with culture, in my opinion, both for those it lifts up to higher plateaus and those it coerces to bow down at its manufactured altar of illusion: such an unnatural and unreal arrangement dehumanizes everyone involved. This is the con of Kubrick, and it is as fascinating and as alluring as the Overlook Hotel.

But also finally, I think, as soul-destroying.

The very idea of greatness, or: Stanley is as Stanley does

> "I was very impressed with Kubrick; he knew all the graphics work I had ever heard of, and probably more."
> —Marvin Minsky, Director of the MIT Computer Science and Artificial Intelligence Laboratory

Why did Kubrick's later films only become recognized as "great" years after their release? Why do people who see them as "great" never talk about the very obvious ways in which they *aren't* great, or even very good, such as Jack Nicholson's scenery-chewing in *The Shining*,[30] how rambling and vacuous *Full Metal Jacket* is, or the excruciatingly inept staging in most of *Eyes Wide Shut*? The only person I know of who has touched on this question at all is the philosopher Slavoj Žižek, who suggests that the orgy scenes in *Eyes Wide Shut* were deliberately devoid of erotic charge. Žižek implies that Kubrick was, in a sense, sacrificing dramatic effect in order to make a thematic point. I think it goes much deeper than this and that both text *and* subtext are incidental to Kubrick's larger goals.

Kubrick's involvement with his films' marketing went as far as measuring the size of the newspaper ads, and in cases when they were smaller than had been paid for, making complaints. So while Kubrick's films are not personal works, in the usual sense of revealing things about his inner life, his personal involvement in them was immense. And, of course, they are almost exclusively talked about in terms of being *Stanley Kubrick* films. My original thesis was that the main thing that makes a Kubrick film "great" is that it is a Kubrick film. I have now amended this thesis to something more nuanced, that the belief in Kubrick as a great filmmaker is essential to how his films are being experienced. Without this belief, a viewer experiences the films quite differently.

The theory explored by researcher Jay Weidner (featured in *Room 237*) that Kubrick was involved in filming phony footage of the 1969 Moon landing also states that all his films after that were not made as ordinary movies but as a *coded confession*. (Rather charmingly, Weidner begins his argument by claiming that Kubrick was bored with making movies after *A Clockwork Orange* and that *Barry Lyndon* is the work of a bored filmmaker.)

Kubrick's later films suggest that Kubrick saw film (and art in general) as a tool for manipulation, deception, exploitation, and for *the imposition of false values*—all of which is consistent with Weidner's theory, without being in any way dependent on it. Whether he was complicit with this covert function of film or whether, as his inarticulate worshippers claim, he was attempting to break the spell by exposing the machinery of the art form, is central to the present work.

Exhibit "A" is *A Clockwork Orange*, Kubrick's first work after *2001* and the Apollo mission. In the film, Kubrick seems to strongly identify with Alex, the psychopath, turning him into the unequivocal hero of the film. In the words of Pauline Kael, he was "sucking up to the thugs in the audience."[31] While this is open to debate, the evidence strongly suggests that Kubrick *did* tailor his film to appeal to a youthful audience (it was a huge hit with teenagers) and that a significant portion of that audience—significant because of how expressive it was—took the film as a kind of incitement to violence, to such an extent, in fact, that Kubrick *prevented the film from being shown after its initial run in his own "neighborhood" (the UK) due to copycat crimes.*

If we allow Kael's statement to stand, why would a visionary artist and intellectual "giant" want to suck up to thugs, and suffer a crisis of conscience about it afterwards?

* * *

> "If you accept the idea that one views a film in a state of 'day-dream,' then this symbolic dreamlike content becomes a powerful factor in influencing your feeling about the film. Since your dreams can take you into areas which can never be part of your conscious mind, I think a work of art can operate on you in much the same way as a dream does."
>
> —Stanley Kubrick, on *A Clockwork Orange*

A Clockwork Orange is a kind of meta-movie. Even as it shows how images of violence condition Alex (Malcolm McDowell) by psychically violating him, Kubrick is doing the same with *his* film's imagery. As if to prove the efficacy of Kubrick's method, the film allegedly caused mimetic crimes after its release in England (where Kubrick had recently moved), as a result of which the director had the film withdrawn from circulation in Britain. Which other filmmaker has ever had the power to *ban* his own work? As far as I know, this has never happened, before or since, in cinema history. (One close parallel can be found in the unsubstantiated rumors that Frank Sinatra pressured United Artists to withdraw *The Manchurian Candidate* after John F. Kennedy's assassination.)

Intended or not, there was one direct result of the film's banning that I can personally testify to: as a teenager growing up in the UK, *A Clockwork Orange* became a minor obsession for me, possessing as it did all the power of forbidden fruit. In retrospect, this was the beginning of my Kubrick obsession. I eventually saw the movie in Paris at about 16. The main appeal of the movie, besides McDowell's performance, was the sexualized violence, particularly the rape in the opening scene, which I found highly arousing, as I think Kubrick meant it to be. So it's fair to say Kubrick successfully catered to *my* inner thug.

As a footnote to this anecdote, it's worth mentioning that my quest to see *A Clockwork Orange* led me—like Bill Harford in *Eyes Wide Shut*—into the darker underbelly of London's porno circuit, looking for a pirate copy of the film. But more on this later.

The works of Satan

> "I think he wants to hurt people with this movie. I think he really wants to make a movie that will hurt people."
> —Stephen King, on *The Shining*

I would like to propose an additional nuance to my already thorny thesis. It is this: the meta-appeal of Kubrick's work for intellectual viewers (I suspect mostly male) is that of being hailed as a great artist *without having to expose anything of one's interior life*, and thereby avoiding the risk of having that inner self rejected. This is Kubrick's "great" accomplishment: like General Jack D. Ripper, Dr. Stanley denies us his essence, and is raised up for it as a great Tantric master rather than the lunatic who kick-started Armageddon.

This is the ego's dream made flesh, and it makes Kubrick a mythical figure of the Satanic kind: a demiurge worshipped for all the wrong reasons.[32]

Kubrick's later films—starting as early as *Dr. Strangelove*, but fully observable with *A Clockwork Orange*—show contempt for audiences, specifically for a certain kind of intellectual, namely, the people Kubrick knew would be the first to embrace the films. And there is a certain kind of intellectual who *admires nothing so much as being regarded with contempt*.

General audiences have never succumbed easily to the Kubrick spell, at least not until the intelligentsia told them to. (This is not necessarily true of *2001: A Space Odyssey* or *A Clockwork Orange*, which were embraced by the counterculture; though even here they may have needed some directing: early reviews of *2001* called it "the ultimate trip movie.") When *Eyes Wide Shut* first came out, for example, it was almost unanimously seen as a bad movie. After a decade or so of "critical reevaluation," it was being talked about as his last masterpiece. Central to Kubrick's mastery is that his films are incomplete until they have been embraced by the intelligentsia and turned into *hierocratic cultural artifacts*, weapons in the canon.

In modern art, there is a semi-secret tradition of making art that is a subtle fuck-you to the buyer, an insult that is only complete when the buyer embraces the work—when he or she "buys it." I think Kubrick's work is "subversive" in this way: not because it is great art but *because it isn't*. In a very subtle and perverse way, Kubrick exposes the falseness of cultural values, but only to those who recognize what he is doing—which judging by the record is almost no one. People either see Kubrick films as great or as not-great; I think they are neither. I don't think they are *films* at all. I think they are tools in a vast, half-century-long psychological experiment.

* * *

"*2001* is said to have caught on with youth (which can make it happen); and it's said that the movie will stone you—which is meant to be a recommendation. Despite a few dissident voices—I've heard it said, for example, that *2001* 'gives you a bad trip because the visuals don't go with the music'—the promotion has been remarkably effective with students. 'The tribes' tune in so fast that college students thousands of miles apart 'have heard'

> what a great trip *2001* is before it has even reached their city …
> The ponderous blurry appeal of the picture may be that it takes
> its stoned audience out of this world to a consoling vision of a
> graceful world of space, controlled by superior godlike minds,
> where the hero is reborn as an angelic baby. It has the dreamy
> somewhere-over-the-rainbow appeal of a new vision of heaven.
> *2001* is a celebration of cop-out."
> —Pauline Kael, "Trash, Art, and the Movies"

The Kubrick film most unanimously agreed to be a work of art is *2001: A Space Odyssey*. Looked at soberly (without dropping acid or drawing on our own bottomless resources of religio-orgiastic fantasies), what's the film about? Essentially, the story of *2001* is this: once we were but apes, but one day an intergalactic intelligence arrived and inspired our simian ancestors with the idea of tool-technology—and of using technology to get ahead (through violence). This alien-assisted evolution eventually led to space travel and artificial intelligence. The alien intelligence, having already prepared it millennia in advance, lured space-faring man, along with AI, into a second encounter.[33]

2001 is about everything (from the Dawn of Man to infinity, and beyond), which is another way of saying it is about nothing. Its premise is so broad that, viewed from a certain angle, it's a bit stupid. Pauline Kael was one of the very few who noticed, calling the film "monumentally unimaginative." Her point of view proved so out of whack with the consensus that it's been largely forgotten. Yet it's possible Kael nailed—in her inimitably irreverent fashion—how the very grandeur of Kubrick's vision proved its paucity. *2001* appeals to the conqueror and the colonizer in us all, while catering to the dissociated, fragmented child that wants to be a star so badly it will kill to get it.

Nonetheless, to say that *2001* is a stupid or unimaginative movie requires some qualifying. It's both highly intelligent *and* kind of dumb, and since we know that neither Kubrick nor Arthur C. Clarke were dummies, it's safe to assume that the obtuseness of the film was intentional, that it was being put in service of the *intelligence* behind it. (John Baxter writes that "Clarke and Kubrick made a match. Both were solitaries by nature. Both had a streak of homoeroticism that favored the sort of film *2001* would become: sleek, sexless, preoccupied with style. Both were opinionated and conceited—Clarke's nickname was 'Ego' … Clarke had been faithful to a boyhood vision of science as savior of mankind, and of mankind as a race of potential gods destined for the stars," Baxter, pp. 203–204).

My question is: did Kubrick *believe* he was telling the greatest story ever told, that he was taking us from the Dawn of Man all the way to infinity and beyond? Or was it only a calculated use of skill and technology—with the assistance of his hidden backers—combined with precise timing (releasing the film at the height of the countercultural movement), to convince the world they had seen something of epic significance? *2001* is a religious fantasy disguised as a scientific parable. But suppose that it's really about how Stanley Kubrick and his invisible backers perfected the science and art of filmmaking as a tool for manipulation, to the degree that they could hoodwink the world and make them believe something that was untrue?

* * *

> "If Stanley Kubrick's *The Shining* is about anything you can be sure of, it's tracking."
>
> —Pauline Kael, "Devolution"

The Shining has all the necessary ingredients to be a hugely entertaining movie. There is no conceivable reason for it to fail as horror entertainment. Yet apparently it fails, hence the almost unanimous disappointment with which it was first received. Yet the film failed in such an unfamiliar way that it created a special kind of fascination, such that I kept revisiting the movie until, eventually, it *worked*! In this way, the film has managed to succeed, over time, and to become for many people something not less enjoyable than horror fiction but more so. Later Kubrick movies (most especially *Eyes Wide Shut*) have attempted the same "stunt." *Eyes Wide Shut* is an extraordinarily bad movie. It is extraordinary because of how bad it is, but also the *ways* in which it is bad: consciously, rationally, intentionally bad. Judging by Kubrick's success, he finally succeeded in causing consciously designed badness to be received, by intellectuals at least, as *greatness*.

What makes Kubrick "greater" than other filmmakers is that his work magnifies a distortion at the core of our culture of personality worship. Kubrick films erase the other in order to make Kubrick's own self-regard complete. A Kubrick film is about "tracking," the eye and mind behind the camera, that is, Kubrick himself. Another way of saying that Kubrick puts nothing of himself into his films (though it sounds like the opposite) is that he empties them of everything that is not-himself. Kubrick may have been the rarest of creatures—though also the most dangerous—a creative nihilist.

Logically, a true nihilist would not create at all; but if he did, he would create films like Kubrick, films which negate values, *not* as a way to liberate us from them but as a means to impose *their own value* on us. In a kind of *Clockwork Orange* conditioning, the central value of Kubrick films is Kubrick himself, i.e., the fact that they *are* Kubrick films, i.e., the value bestowed upon them by the Kubrick brand. They are objects of self-worship that, like Lucifer or the Monolith, demand worship from the other. Simply put, the subject of every Kubrick film is Stanley Kubrick. Not Kubrick the man—Kubrick is the anti-Woody Allen in this regard—but Kubrick the artist, the filmmaker, the visionary genius.

7. IRONICALLY, THIS IS ONE OF THE HIDDEN NARRATIVES OF THE SHINING RECOGNIZED EQUALLY BY BOTH SCHOOL/MATRIX 1 + 2: THE KUBRICK/KING WELTANSCHAUUNGSKRIEG

8. SINCE IT'S WELL KNOWN THAT KUBRICK, THE GENIUS FILMMAKER, "PULLED RANK" ON KING, THE PULP WRITER, THE FACT ONE OF THE FEW ON-SET SHOTS OF THE SHINING CREW MADE PUBLIC INCLUDES A SIGN SAYING "DEFINITLEY NO KING" IS SURELY A PIECE OF EVIDENCE EVEN THE STAIDEST STUDENTS OF THE FIRST, "NOTHING TO DECLARE BUT HIS GENIUS" SCHOOL WOULD BE HARD-PRESSED TO DENY? PROOF THAT KUBRICK ENJOYED PLANTING HIDDEN CLUES IN HIS WORK IN ORDER TO COMMUNICATE MESSAGES INDEPENDENTLY OF THE PRIMARY NARRATIVE!

+ HERE IS THE BRIDGE BETWEEN 1st + 2nd MATRIX-SCHOOLS - YET ALSO A LIMINAL SPACE THAT BELONGS TO NEITHER

CHAPTER 3

Crossing the Kubrickon

Under the seat

"I don't know what led me to make any of my films."
—Stanley Kubrick

It was via my adolescent infatuation for violent movies—when *A Clockwork Orange* was near the top of my "must-see" movies—that I first became aware of how sensitive my father was to violence. I already knew he was a pacifist, because it ran in the family: his own father co-designed the now famous peace symbol for the Campaign for Nuclear Disarmament (possibly a front for the Fabian Society—but that's another story). Presumably, in response to my own growing passion, my father told me one day (and several times after) how much he disliked violent movies, specifically by citing *A Clockwork Orange*.

"I was so terrified when I saw it," he said, "that I ended up under the seat."

Of course, this only intensified my desire to see the film. At the same time, it caused a feeling of antipathy in me toward my father, and for many years after I regarded his distaste for film violence as moral squeamishness. I even said as much in my introduction to *The Blood*

Poets, though without mentioning him directly (knowing he would read it, which he did).

In the context of *The Kubrickon*, this memory takes on a very different flavor and meaning. What I was being made aware of, via my father's memory of *Orange*, was an early clue to the hidden design behind Kubrick's films, namely, that they were designed as part of an experiment which included *observing the responses of audience members*.

This idea was confirmed for me when I saw the 2008 documentary *Stanley Kubrick's Boxes*. Among the thousands of boxes full of research material which Kubrick left behind after his death was a meticulously filed collection of fan letters. The letters had been organized, by Kubrick, into positive, negative, and "crank," arranged alphabetically according to the location of the letter's writer. Kubrick's personal assistant, Tony Frewin, explained: "[Kubrick] thought, I may need a spy, I may need an agent [in any given location] so he had a name and number."

The interviewer, Jon Ronson, offers an innocuous explanation—to check on a print of *The Shining* that was showing in that particular town. "It could be something entirely different," Frewin replies with a shake of his head. "He saw those as potential agents in the field. *Stanley's irregulars*."

The reference is to Sherlock Holmes, another Aspergerian genius.

* * *

> "Is a work of art possible if pseudoscience and the technology of movie-making become more important to the 'artist' than man?"
> —Pauline Kael, "Trash, Art, and the Movies"

According to *A Clockwork Orange* author Anthony Burgess, the Nadsat language which he invented for his novella "was meant to turn *A Clockwork Orange* into *a brainwashing primer*. You should read the book and at the end you should find yourself in possession of a minimal Russian vocabulary—without effort, with surprise."[34]

As previously mentioned, the ultra-violence of Kubrick's film version was blamed by the media for inciting a string of copycat crimes, stories such as: a woman raped by assailants performing "Singing in the Rain," gangs of thugs in England dressed up as droogs, a 16-year-old obsessed with the film who beat a 60-year-old tramp to death, and so on.

Most strikingly of all, Arthur Bremer, the attempted assassin of American presidential candidate George Wallace, wrote in his diary on

May 1, 1972: "saw *Clockwork Orange*, & thought about getting Wallace all through the picture—fantasing [sic] myself as the Alek [sic] on the screen come to real life …"[35] On May 14, he shot Wallace, paralyzing him for life.

(May 1 was the last day of Jack Torrance's stint as caretaker of the Overlook Hotel; traditionally, May Day is a day to make a sacrificial offering. Bremer's diary was an inspiration for Paul Schrader when he wrote the script for *Taxi Driver*. *Taxi Driver* "inspired" Ronald Reagan's attempted assassin, John Hinckley Jr. Unlike *Clockwork Orange*, *Taxi Driver* is a film as close to my own heart as any film I have seen.)

Once the final stage of this experiment was completed (*Eyes Wide Shut*), Kubrick was withdrawn from the field (via his death, real or otherwise, natural or induced), in order for the second stage to begin. The second stage involves not merely the reevaluation of his films *but a growing number of increasingly bizarre and idiosyncratic, obsessive-immersive analyses.*

Like Ozymandias in *Watchmen*, Kubrick, alive or dead (and/or the agencies behind him) could (via the internet) collate, sift, sort, and analyze the endless stream of data being generated by these myriad obsessive quests for supposed meanings, patterns, correspondences, and intentions hidden within the Master's oeuvre. And as with Ozymandias, there is no way to determine if Kubrick's intelligence was of the benevolent kind or not. The line between *hubris* and divine fiat is one only the gods can see. By his fruit shall ye know him.

I have until now judged Kubrick on the fruit of the movies and accordingly have judged him harshly. But before we can judge Kubrick *or* his movies, we have to look at another fruit: that of the films' advocates. By advocates, I refer not to the sap-headed intelligentsia who raised Kubrick up to the throne of Grand Master of Cinema. These are the most deceived of all. (In the closing line of *Kubrick: A Life in Pictures*, Christiane Kubrick says how Kubrick, when asked how he was doing, would often joke, "Still fooling 'em.") No, the Kubrick advocates whose experience has *juice* are not the sap-headed intelligentsia or the ordinary Kubrick fans (if there is such an animal), but those basement-dwelling obsessives featured in *Room 237* who have willingly put themselves inside Kubrick's labyrinth and faced down the Minotaur, in their mad quest for meaning inside a meaningless creation. They are the caretakers of the Kubrickon, and it is with them that the real truth lies—even if they haven't found it yet.

Judging by *Room 237*, a movie I found more enjoyable than any of Kubrick's works, there is some juicy fruit here indeed—and plenty of mechanical oranges too. Though the final results are not yet in, a naked emperor is a lot more interesting than an imaginary metal jacket. And like it or not, through the process of writing this book and uncovering this metanarrative, this liminalist text, I have joined the ranks of the caretakers.

At which point, the voice of my inner editor inevitably intones: *you have always been the caretaker, Jake.*

The Overlook, again

> "Forget the wax and feathers, and do a better job on the wings."
> —Stanley Kubrick, final speech

Some years before he made *The Shining*, Kubrick spent months of his life, probably years, preparing a film about Napoleon. One of the actors he considered for the main role was Jack Nicholson. The film never happened. Instead, ten years later, they made *The Shining* about a petty despot ruling over his family.

(One of the propositions Jay Weidner makes is that the deal Kubrick cut with the US government, when he agreed to film the staged Moon landings, included *carte blanche* to make any film he wanted after that. His failure to make "Napoleon" would seem to give the lie to this. On the other hand, the professed reason Kubrick abandoned the project was the release of *Waterloo*, which included a Napoleon plotline, at exactly the time he was gearing up to make his own film, as it were poisoning the well from which Kubrick was hoping to drink. The same thing had almost happened with *Dr. Strangelove*: when Kubrick got wind that a movie was underway based on *Fail-Safe*, a novel by Eugene Burdick and Harvey Wheeler, he and *Red Alert* author Peter George instigated a lawsuit against it, delaying its release until six months after that of *Strangelove*. Kubrick was not so lucky with his Holocaust movie, *The Aryan Papers*: by the time he was ready to begin production, Spielberg's *Schindler's List* had been released and Kubrick abandoned the film. What better way to clip Kubrick's wings without actually breaking the terms of the deal? It is curious, if so, that Kubrick then handed over the reins of *AI* to Spielberg, and produced the film for him. In fact, it's curious that Kubrick formed an alliance with Spielberg at all, because their artistic sensibilities could hardly be further apart.)

Kubrick went from the highest aspiration—a historical epic about a great warrior—to the lowest, a pulp horror yarn about ghosts and psychic powers. One possible reading of the oddly "off" tone of *The Shining* is that Kubrick was communicating his contempt for the material he was adapting—not only in his flagrant disregard for the Stephen King novel but also in how he subtly (and not-so-subtly) sabotages his film by "aping" the worst effects of horror fiction: the overwrought, sometimes campy imagery, the crashing and relentless music, and the kabuki of Nicholson's performance.[36] (In a French interview Kubrick gave around the release of *Full Metal Jacket*, Kubrick expressed a different view, that he was drawn to the novel for its powerful storyline and that he had always been interested in psychism. He gives no indication that making *The Shining* was an ignominious choice for him.)

Whether or not Kubrick was communicating his contempt for the source material he was working with, Stephen King at least thought so: he has railed against the film for four decades. But if Kubrick wasn't really trying to make a horror movie—if he deliberately got it wrong as a way to signal that he didn't give a damn about King's novel or the horror genre—what *was* he doing?

In King's novel, the Torrances drive a red beetle; in Kubrick's film, it is yellow. In *Room 237*, Jay Weidner points out how, on his way to the Overlook to be killed, Halloran (Scatman Crothers) passes a car accident on the road: a red Volkswagen beetle has been crushed by a truck. Weidner claims this is a clear signal to King that Kubrick has consciously wrecked his vehicle (the book) and replaced it with his own. If so, King apparently got the message. When he expressed his contempt for Kubrick's film, he used the same metaphor and called it a fancy car "with no engine." Even more weirdly, some years later, in June 1999 (three months after Kubrick died), King—who made his own directorial debut in 1986 with a tawdry little horror movie about demonic trucks—was very nearly killed, on the highway outside his house, when he was run over by a minivan.

There is another movie beneath the garish surface of *The Shining*; this second movie is not so much a movie as *a blueprint*, a blueprint for our psychic imprisonment inside the physical universe, as specifically represented by Kubrick's own imprisonment, both within the military-entertainment complex of "Hollywood" (which sabotaged his Napoleon project and drove him into gaudy pulp like *The Shining*), and in the horror genre he was forced to use to get his message across. Moving outward several steps from this more local perspective reveals a more "Gnostic" blueprint, namely, that of the soul's imprisonment within a false reality by "the Archons," the rulers of the physical universe.

There is a moment in *The Shining* in which Wendy and Danny are exploring the garden maze outside the Overlook Hotel while Jack, failing to write again, stands over a model of the maze inside the hotel (the hotel is also a maze) and looks down on the tiny figures of his wife and son, captive inside an artificial construct. This is a non-realistic moment in the film, but it is also thematically inconsistent. Jack Torrance is not a godlike figure, by any stretch of the imagination, either in his own life or that of his wife and child.

The film's ending (both the climax and the codex) makes clear that *Jack* is the one trapped inside the maze, a prisoner of the labyrinth, frozen in time. So who is the Jack Torrance we see looking down on the maze? One answer is that it is Kubrick, in a moment of *deus ex machina*, having entered into the narrative of his own fiction, tipping his hand. An evil deity, a prison guard, watching with dark fascination as the rats he has lured into his maze wander hopelessly about.

Yet, if Jack Torrance *is* Stanley Kubrick, this is really only a wishful fantasy. Stanley-as-Jack is imagining what it would be like to be on the outside of the labyrinth of illusion, looking in, but apparently he is only able to do so from the point of view of a cruel and sadistic prison keeper.

The "final" answer?

> "You're going into areas where reason doesn't help."
> —Stanley Kubrick

Having written Part I up to this point, while readying to round up my thesis, I had a dream. In the dream, I had been invited by Stanley Kubrick to stay at the Overlook Hotel with him and his family while he shot *The Shining*. Kubrick was confirming to me the idea that he was embedding imagery into the film meant to function as *neuro-linguistic programming* (NLP) for viewers. In the dream, the imagery Stanley showed me was never meant to make it onto the screen but was part of the fictional narrative. It was a drawing of a black man's face on the inside of the door to the office where Jack Torrance has his interview, at the start of the film. The image was put there to sow a subliminal seed in Jack's psyche that *the black man* (Hallorann) was the intended sacrifice (perhaps so that when Jack heard about the former caretaker murdering his wife and child he would unconsciously reach for some other possible victim, and come up with "the black man").

In the dream, I was amazed by the realization that I had failed to mention being in direct communication with Kubrick in my current writing, as if leaving out a minor detail. The dream came on the heels of a waking realization. Having all but finished Part I, I remembered a similar liminalist essay I wrote about Philip K. Dick, and how, by the end of it, I began to entertain the possibility that I was in psychic communion with Dick. This realization—or fancy—became the underlying meaning of the piece. Now I was making a Kubrick-esque list of bullet points to round up with, and it seemed as though the same thing was happening with Kubrick!

And now for those bullet points.

1. Stanley Kubrick was less an artist than a scientist.
2. Kubrick approached each of his films in the early years as an experiment.
3. *The Killing* was a conventional filmmaking experiment—how to make a heist film with an existential theme and a fragmented timeline.
4. *Paths of Glory* was a way to test how far he could challenge the military establishment and accepted ideas about patriotism: the film was banned in France (bullseye).

5. *Spartacus* was an experiment in studio filmmaking, enough to establish Kubrick's name and convince him never to do it again. It's also been suggested that Kubrick intended to break the Hollywood anti-Communist blacklist with the film. Both the original writer (Howard Fast) and the screenwriter (Dalton Trumbo) were blacklisted communists, and Trumbo's secret identity was finally revealed with *Spartacus*. "When *Spartacus* was released as a film written by Dalton Trumbo, the blacklist was officially broken just as Kubrick had hoped ... *Spartacus* won four academy awards and brought in more money to Universal Studios than any film in its history."[37]
6. *Lolita* took on what remains in some ways the most delicate and disturbing subject matter we know of, pedophilia, and was censored by the Catholic League of Decency (Kubrick got the attention of the Pope).
7. *Dr. Strangelove* experimented both with audience reaction and political power by making a film about (surely) the most serious subject of all: the destruction of the human race, all the while aiming for laughs. It was also an experiment on how well he could simulate the inner workings of the military-industrial complex. Allegedly he had John F. Kennedy's support on the film, and its release came close on the heels of the Cuban missile crisis. (The original premiere was November 22, 1963, but it was canceled due to JFK's assassination.) According to some sources, Kubrick recreated the inside of a B52 bomber so well that he got the attention of the Pentagon, which may have led to his biggest gig yet (one he would never get credit for): faking the Moon landing.
8. *2001: A Space Odyssey* was both an artistic experiment and a sociological one: it targeted the growing counterculture and gave them "the ultimate trip," fueling the LSD craze and the budding new mysticism. And this time, improbably, Kubrick got the Pope's blessing! (The film was chosen by the Vatican Film Library as one of the 45 most important films of the 20th century and placed first in the special section of artistic works.)
9. Later, from *2001* on, Kubrick's films formed individual but inseparable parts of *a larger experiment* which continued until his death, and beyond.
10. Kubrick is not "one of us." He is "the Man"—the man every aspiring artist aspires to be. He achieved the highest status within the art form, recognized by some as the highest art form of the 20th century.

He was "the Greatest Filmmaker, i.e., Artist, of All Time." (In fact, he is the Wizard of Oz.)
11. Many things in Kubrick's movies, from *2001* on, are deliberately "off." One of the things Kubrick was constantly testing was "How much can I get away with?"
12. Kubrick's films are *impersonal*; they do not appear to show the working out of a personal obsession, as the works of great artists almost invariably do, but nor are they hack-jobs. They are *ultra*-personal in terms of the choices of material and Kubrick's commitment to it.
13. Kubrick's films create cognitive dissonance through ways both apparent and concealed, at levels textual, sub-textual, and "meta" (i.e., in the real world).
14. One primary goal of Kubrick's movies was to elevate his name to the highest cultural plateau. This was not (merely) from personal vanity but strategically, in order to imbue his films with a special quality for viewers that they would otherwise have lacked. (This may be partly why he took longer and longer between films.)
15. The above (point 14) is part of the subtler form of cognitive dissonance which Kubrick strived for. His films were seen to be works of genius because he was established in the consensus view as an unimpeachable genius. Yet they became increasingly incoherent, shapeless, mechanical, forcing an ever greater degree of dissembling and denial on the part of his admirers.
16. Kubrick films are not films but means for experimenting on audiences. They are disguised to look like movies to make it past the audience's defenses. This disguise became less and less important to Kubrick as the experiment progressed.
17. Secrecy severely impedes artistic expression. Kubrick knew this, and rather than try and work against it, he went with it. This is why and how he effectively gave up being an artist with *2001* and became a scientist instead. (Granting that science and art are not mutually exclusive disciplines, but shades on a larger spectrum—one that includes religion, politics, and "magic," or the occult—what I imply here is a shift of *emphasis*.)
18. The incoherent surface of his movies was designed to lure viewers into looking beyond the surface, into the details.
19. Those who don't look but stay on the surface are being "programmed" via a kind of neuro-cinematic programming (NCP). Those who go beyond the surface then enter into a "second matrix."

20. The coded meanings within Kubrick films are largely irrelevant. The only clue that matters in Kubrick's oeuvre is *the fact that people obsessively look for clues*. Kubrick's films generate obsession—for a reason.
21. Kubrick's partial goal was to create a replica of the physical universe with his movies as *a trap for human consciousness*. At the same time, by showing how we let our awareness become trapped, his movies also have the potential (maybe) for alerting us to that trap.
22. Beyond these possibilities or congruent with them, Kubrick was using his movies as the means *to "recruit" human consciousness for an experiment*.
23. Kubrick was not interested in making entertainment, but neither was he interested in making art. He had a very different and more "serious," socio-political and scientific goal.
24. Kubrick consciously gathered data on his fans via their fan letters. These were referred to as his "spies," "agents," and "irregulars." What he used these agents for has never been divulged.
25. Kubrick was aware of the idea of a "holographic universe" in which the part contains the whole. He believed that total immersion in the minutiae of the physical universe is the best, perhaps the only, way to move consciousness beyond the surface into the core of existence.
26. With his obsession-generating movies and his many "agents," all working together on a grand, decades-long experiment, Kubrick was attempting something. What was it? To crack the riddle of the universe and escape the illusory realm of spacetime, to sneak past the Archons to freedom? This was my first thought, but on consideration, I decided it was too much like a movie script, and therefore just one more layer of the Kubrickon—the second matrix—designed to generate yet more obsession.
27. The answer, then, is that Kubrick was attempting something else, the biggest clues to which can be found both in his most famous film, and in his last, unrealized film project.

Of course, this is all completely speculative. It is easily as improbable as Weidner's argument that Kubrick faked the Moon landings, and even harder to prove. I am not going to attempt to prove it, however, since that would be tedious and ultimately futile. I only wish to outline the reasoning by which I ended up staring at this wild improbability and, following the counsel of Sherlock Holmes, accepting it, tentatively (or liminally), as *the best interpretation of the facts*.

We currently have a wide array of technology for a working interface between brain function (which is at least one primary aspect of human consciousness) and computers. Microchips can embed memories into the brains of Alzheimer's patients so they won't get lost. Eyesight can be improved through similar implants, even restored. There is evidence (mostly confined to the annals of conspiracy lore) of the possibility of turning radio waves into brain waves and transmitting voices into people's heads. Less controversial, brain–computer–interface (BCI) technology now allows the movement of a cursor on a screen by "thought" (whatever thought is—in this case, presumably electrical signals from the brain; in Melbourne, scientists "managed to connect a human brain to a Windows 10 computer by threading a wire through a blood vessel").[38]

At the same time, the recent discoveries regarding mirror neurons indicate the degree to which an individual's brain state communicates unconsciously, not merely via spoken language but even written language. Telepathy, as Kubrick's long-time nemesis Stephen King wrote (in *On Writing*), is an ancient reality that is only now being recognized by science. It is not occultism but a hidden function of physiology. Brain states. The more immersed a person is in the material, the more their synapses start firing, the more their consciousness bleeds into whatever they are focused on, charging it with the sort of intensity that Dostoyevsky gave to *Crime and Punishment*—or that an obsessive basement dweller gives to his *Shining* exegesis.

It's been remarked on how *2001: A Space Odyssey* was remarkably prescient science fiction in terms of the development of technology in every way but one—the creation of artificial intelligence. Almost 50 years after the film came out, we are *apparently* not much closer to creating a sentient machine. I disagree, but that's the thesis of this book, or part of it.

Creation can't come out of nothing: *ex nihilo nihil fit*. While the machine might be a matrix for intelligence to be born through, that still leaves the question of how to *seed* the technological womb. The answer—the answer Kubrick came up with and was attempting via his movies, from *2001* on—is *to seed it with human consciousness itself*.

The third phase of the Kubrickon is happening now, via the internet and a thousand or a hundred thousand of Kubrick's irregulars, together and apart, "obsessing" over the minutiae of his movies and inventing a potentially endless series of correspondences and arrangements, theorems and exegeses, by which to make sense of the Master's oeuvre and bring coherence to it.

The internet is becoming a matrix to receive all of this immersive psychic energy—all of these humming brainwaves—and focus them into a single multi-faceted creative expression. It is the fusion of human consciousness with both the digital imagery of the films themselves and then, since the message is also the medium, with the computer software that houses it (if not the hardware), with the final goal of making it *conscious*.

Kubrick's work is designed to this end, to get as many synapses as possible firing and focused into a single field (Kubrick-mania), and fuel the engine of artificial intelligence.

Not *deus ex machina* but God *into* the machine.

A two-way mirror

"There is a non-verbal form of communication."
—Stanley Kubrick

Kubrick's overriding interest—as a man with an alleged IQ of 200—was problem-solving. This is what drew him to movie-making, which is a constant process of encountering and solving problems. In 1966 (just say), he was presented with a problem of epic proportions: how to fake a Moon landing and deceive the world.

2001 was Kubrick's attempt to solve the problem of narrative, to make a movie that wouldn't be restricted by dramatic conventions such as linearity or coherence. By this time, Kubrick had attained such power and freedom within the industry (a power no other filmmaker has ever possessed, before or since) that making movies no longer presented a problem to him—it was no longer sufficient as a challenge to his intellect. But while working on *2001*—researching the science behind the fiction to achieve the greatest authenticity possible—Kubrick encountered a problem more suitably scaled to his abilities (and ambitions): AI.

Kubrick's interest, or obsession, with mind control is apparent in how it forms the subject, or at least a major element, of all his movies post-*2001* (with the possible exception of *Barry Lyndon*). This points to Kubrick's prevailing desire to understand the nature of human consciousness, what constitutes free will, self-awareness, and sentience, as opposed to purely mechanical function. Simply put, the preoccupation bleeding through all of Kubrick's movies—from *A Clockwork Orange* to *Eyes Wide Shut*—with how human consciousness can be reduced to a series of mechanisms—pre-programmed behaviors—is like *a scrying mirror* in which he hoped to divine *how a machine might be made conscious*.

CROSSING THE KUBRICKON   49

This is the problem Stanley Kubrick devoted his life to solving.

* * *

> "Anthony Burgess believed that Kubrick's interest in codes led him to 'create relationships without knowing it—like in *2001*, where the name of HAL was associated with IBM. He was totally unaware of it.'"
> —John Baxter, *Stanley Kubrick*[39]

So the plot thickens. If Kubrick was using his movies about mind control *as a form of mind control*, was he trying to explore—by testing—the relationship between artifact and consciousness? Was this how he literally took the art of filmmaking into the realm of science, with the audience member's psyche as his laboratory? And was his real goal, not to experiment on human consciousness, but to discover the possibility of making the relationship *two-way*, to find out if, just as movies affected human consciousness, human consciousness could affect movies—*changing them via the act of seeing them*?

This might seem like an irrational, counterintuitive leap; yet it also has a peculiar kind of logic. Why *wouldn't* the relationship between consciousness and artifice be two-way? Isn't that the very meaning of "relationship"? (To autistics, objects are often experienced as sentient, and ancient animistic culture viewed the physical world as directly interfacing with human consciousness and therefore having its own kind of consciousness. Kubrick was particularly interested in *The Golden Bough*, about magical beliefs in previous cultures.)

By planting enough seemingly anomalous but subtly meaningful (or deliberately meaningless) touches in his films, Kubrick's aim was to capture the attention of viewers *just below the threshold of consciousness*. When something in our environment doesn't fit, the brain notices it and stores it as an "unidentified element." This is a very deeply programmed survival function (based in the reptilian brain), because anything in the environment that hasn't been identified remains *a possible threat*, and so the brain keeps going back to it to try and figure out what it is. A movie is a virtual environment that consciousness enters into like a maze at a sensory level (the brain can't tell the difference). In just the same way, people go back to Kubrick movies again and again to try and figure out the anomalies and put to rest the tension of not knowing.[40]

Once this mechanism has been activated, it has the potential to become automatic. If Kubrick places enough meaningful anomalies in his films, the brain becomes alert to them and starts finding them where they *aren't*—or at least finding anomalies that Kubrick didn't consciously put there. The real world is full of such anomalies and a movie set is also part of the real world; there's another function of the brain that not only seeks to identify anomalous elements but also *creates meaning and context* for them, even where they can't find it. It is known as *pareidolia*:

> a psychological phenomenon involving a vague and random stimulus (often an image or sound) being perceived as significant. Common examples include seeing images of animals or faces in clouds, the man in the moon or the Moon rabbit, and hearing hidden messages on records when played in reverse. The word comes from the Greek words para (παρά, "beside, alongside, instead") in this context meaning something faulty, wrong, instead of; and the noun eidōlon (εἴδωλον "image, form, shape") the diminutive of eidos. Pareidolia is a type of apophenia, seeing patterns in random data ... Combined with Apophenia and hierophany (a manifestation of the sacred), pareidolia may have helped early societies organize chaos and make the world intelligible.
>
> (Wikipedia)

Kubrick was a man who amassed vast amounts of data on any given project before proceeding. If he set about to help create a working form of artificial intelligence in 1968, and spent the next 30 years working on this project—*using his movies as the primary means to achieve it*—you can bet he did his research.

Kubrick's intelligence was such that he intuited, as far back as 1968, that the presumed means for creating artificial intelligence would never work. There was no way to bring God out of a machine because God was not there. So God would have to be put *into* the machine. Just as he approached his art scientifically, Kubrick approached the ultimate scientific problem as an artist—a creator, a modern Prometheus. (Kubrick was every bit as much Baron Frankenstein as the Wizard of Oz.)

It was not enough to build the perfect edifice. It would have to be also inhabited, the dead flesh animated. Like the Overlook in winter, the Kubrickon would need a caretaker.

Not just one, but legion.

PART II

AGENT STANLEY

"Stanley is like a vampire of people's brains."
—Adrienne Corri

CHAPTER 4

How the solar system was won

"It's a bad, bad sign when a movie director begins to think of himself as a myth-maker, and this limp myth of a grand plan that justifies slaughter and ends with resurrection has been around before. Kubrick's storyline—accounting for evolution by an extraterrestrial intelligence—is probably the most gloriously redundant plot of all time."
—Pauline Kael, "Trash, Art, and the Movies"

The first Kubrick movie I saw was undoubtedly *Spartacus*. It was just the sort of movie (along with *Ben Hur*) that I would have watched as a pre-adolescent, pre-Eastwood kid. Maybe it was on a Saturday evening with my mother and siblings, or maybe a Sunday afternoon with my father (not entirely beyond the bounds of the possible). *Spartacus* is the one movie—even counting his early pulp work—that Kubrick made as a director-for-hire and the work that bears the least obvious Kubrick stamp. I remember my father saying, at least once but probably more, that he thought *Spartacus* was Kubrick's best movie. Did he say it in tandem with saying how unpleasant he found *A Clockwork Orange*? Or was the context his sympathy with slave revolts (he was ostensibly a socialist, though as the head of a multinational corporation, his social positioning was far from anti-establishment)? Whatever the case, it has only occurred to me now, 40 years later, while working on this book, that he may have been deliberately *dissing* Stanley by favoring the one movie Kubrick considered a blight (if not a tactical error) on his curriculum vitae (not counting his juvenilia, which he later suppressed).

By saying "I think *Spartacus* is his best movie," or words to that effect, my father was signaling to me that he had little time or interest for Kubrick's more "artistic" aspirations. Maybe this was where and how my own skepticism began. Of only a handful of conversations I can remember having with my father—at least with such specific content—only a fraction of them were about movies. And yet, *two* of them were about Kubrick movies: one in which he communicated his hatred of screen violence, with *Orange* as Exhibit A, the other with faint praise that damned all Stanley's bids for greatness by placing them in second place to his one piece of studio hackwork. Is a theme emerging?

The anomaly of Kubrick's optimistic vision of the future of man

> "The secondary title of *Dr. Strangelove*, which we took to be satiric, *How I Learned to Stop Worrying and Love the Bomb*, was not, it now appears, altogether satiric for Kubrick. *2001* celebrates the invention of tools of death, as an evolutionary route to a higher order of non-human life. Kubrick literally learned to stop worrying and love the bomb; he's become his own butt—the Herman Kahn of extraterrestrial games theory."
>
> —Pauline Kael, "Trash, Art, and the Movies"

In his Kubrick biography (called, typically, *Stanley Kubrick*), John Baxter notes that film critic David Austen tried to write his own book on Kubrick, working with film writer Peter Cowie (who wrote a biography of Francis Coppola). Austen fell ill and was replaced by Neil Hornick, who was in contact with Kubrick about the book. The condition for Kubrick's co-operation was that nothing would be published without Kubrick's approval. Making the agreement official, Kubrick's lawyer gave Cowie a document to sign, giving Kubrick "wide powers of veto." Kubrick "wasn't satisfied with Cowie's attempts to provide an objective standard in relation to 'valid criticism.' *The publisher would have to rely on Kubrick to be fair*" (emphasis added).

Cowie's manuscript was rejected, not for any factual errors but "because your chapter on each film gives [Kubrick and his lawyers] the impression of a 'mixed review,' a summary of the bad points, which, in his view, almost always outweigh the good." Cowie attempted to publish it elsewhere, but those publishers were "threatened with legal action ... Shortly after, Alexander Walker's *Stanley Kubrick Directs* appeared, assessing the films in a sunny and uncritical light" (all quotes Baxter, p. 298). Mission accomplished.

As far as I know, the case of a filmmaker litigating against a critic for being too *critical* of his films is unique to Kubrick, and it suggests one of two things. Either a) Kubrick possessed a very fragile ego, harbored deep insecurities about himself as an artist, and was so desperately in need of validation that he couldn't bear negative criticism. Or b) establishing an unimpeachable reputation as a filmmaker was part of a larger strategy, the success of which depended on quashing negative criticism wherever possible. Or both. As Kubrick's publicity director on *2001* Roger Caras put it, "Stanley will deny anything, no matter what, he will deny anything he thinks will reflect less than sensationally on the mythic Kubrick" (Benson, p. 422).

Whatever else this proves, this does confirm an intuitive sense—which I had from a very early age—that there was a kind of conspiracy to create a *false consensus* around Kubrick's work, assigning it a cultural value disproportionate to its merits. On the other hand, there aren't really *any* books on specific filmmaker careers that aren't slanted toward a positive, even fawning, perspective; so maybe this is just business as usual for behind-the-scenes Hollywood (where image is everything). Kubrick's legend being so bloated and exaggerated would only make this more observable.[41]

The Kubrick movie that cemented his reputation, and that remains to this day the cornerstone of his career, is *2001: A Space Odyssey*. Yet the film is a clear anomaly in Kubrick's oeuvre insofar as it presents an optimistic vision of the future of mankind. Kubrick is a filmmaker best known for his bleak, pessimistic, nihilistic vision of human nature and society. In *Dr. Strangelove*, humanity destroys itself out of rank ignorance, paranoia, and runaway delusion (and it is all a joke). In *A Clockwork Orange*, the vicious thug who rapes, tortures, and kills for a smile is the most human character in the film, a babe in the woods compared to the society that "reforms" him. In *Barry Lyndon*, a vacuous social climber attempts to establish himself with the ruling class and progresses steadily in emptiness and ennui until nothing is left but a soulless husk. In *The Shining*, a father goes insane and murders his family, over and over again, for eternity. And so on.

This raises the question as to how it was possible for the man who made these films to believe in *2001*'s message. *Did* he believe it, and if not, what was he intending to communicate? And is this congruent with why so many admire it, including (or especially) other filmmakers? Do those who believe Kubrick was a subversive artist ruthlessly critiquing and exposing corrupt power structures and human folly on the planet, do they also believe in the star child and the transcendent destiny of Man depicted in *2001*?

As John Baxter wrote, "The immediate inspiration for *2001* wasn't science fiction, but the American West." Surprising as it is, this statement makes perfect sense. *How the West was Won* was a 1962 film, 162 mins long, with four directors, that included documentary footage and was shot in "three-panel Cinerama." "All over the world, entrepreneurs who, with studio encouragement, had built or rebuilt cinemas to accommodate Cinerama, demanded films to show in them. Kubrick would sell *2001* to MGM as part of that product." The working title was "How the Solar System was Won" (Baxter, p. 202).

Theft as art

"Kubrick's inspirational banality about how we will become as gods through machinery [is] big-shot show-business deep thinking. This isn't a new show-business phenomenon; it belongs to the genius tradition of the theater. Big entrepreneurs, producers, and directors who stage big spectacular shows, even designers of large sets have traditionally begun to play the role of visionaries and thinkers and men with answers. They get too big for art. Is a work of art possible if pseudoscience and the technology of movie-making become more important to the 'artist' than man? This is central to the failure of *2001*. It's a monumentally unimaginative movie … The light-show trip is of no great distinction; compared to the work of experimental filmmakers like Jordan Belson, it's third-rate. If big film directors are to get credit for doing badly what others have been doing brilliantly for years

> with no money, just because they've put it on a big screen, then businessmen are greater than poets and theft is art."
> —Pauline Kael, "Trash, Art, and the Movies"

We now know that NASA was involved—at least from the 1960s—in using popular arts and media to promote the idea of space travel. This is from William M. Brown and Herman Kahn's "Long-Term Prospects For Developments in Space (A Scenario Approach)":

> The basic purpose of this report is to formulate some useful and interesting images of the long-term future of space, and to encourage and facilitate the use of such images and scenarios by NASA in its studies, planning, and public information programs. We realize that NASA already makes use of scenarios in its planning functions, but the deliberate formulation of long-term scenarios and "images of the future" *has usually been left to outside freelance writers*. We believe it is quite useful, perhaps important, for NASA to intervene in this process and also to facilitate it ... Long-term scenarios about space development, and, even more important, shared images of the future of space, can contribute to a sense of community, of institutional meaning and purpose, of high morale, and even—to use somewhat extravagant terms—of manifest destiny or of "religious" mission ... Such images can have a great impact on political issues—both internal and external.
>
> (Brown and Kahn, 1977, pp. 1–2, emphasis added)

Two years before *2001* was released, it was already being sold as something more than a work of fantasy entertainment. In the 1966 documentary, "*2001: A Space Odyssey*—A Look Behind the Future," the narrator informs us that "The coming century will reveal a new and startling universe ... This is the promise of *2001*." The documentary praises motion pictures' "ability to educate while entertaining," then announces a special issue of *Look* magazine devoted to "the social impact of celestial exploration ... timed to ride the crest of MGM's multimillion dollar promotional program." It then pitches to the magazine's advertisers as "direct beneficiaries" of this program:

This will afford you a unique publishing vehicle for projecting your corporate future plans. Your message will appear against an educational backdrop revealing how all segments of American industry are anticipating the opportunities and the need of tomorrow's world, offering the public the information needed to make an affirmative judgment on the great national investment required to continue this progress.

(Evidently, an affirmative response is the only correct one to this "information.")

The narrator then quotes (ex-Nazi) Wernher von Braun on how there are more than 400,000 men and women, 20,000 companies, and 150 universities working with NASA alone, and that more than 95 percent of NASA's budget goes to contractors. Lastly, he compares Jefferson's purchase of Louisiana for 15 percent of gross national product at that time to today, when NASA's budget is only 1 percent of our gross national product—the implication being that the space program is criminally underfunded. Keir Dullea (Bowman in *2001*) describes Kubrick as "one of the giants," and his own character as "a gigantic figure." Astronauts, he says, are "the heroes of our time."

Arthur C. Clarke's goldfish bowl

"Project Icarus is about more than just designing a vehicle. It is also about keeping the vision of humans in space alive for our generation and the next; a necessary requirement if we are to move forward incrementally towards the stars."

—"Creating a Self-Fulfilling Prophecy," Icarus Interstellar

Much of this underlying ideology can be blamed on the film's author, Arthur C. Clarke, a highly connected government insider and self-professed lover of children.[42] Clarke was certainly a believer in advocating space conquest, and he probably did as much as any single figure to promote it. But Clarke and Kubrick worked closely together and by all accounts were perfectly compatible as a team. So what about Clarke's history? Clarke found work as a civil servant in London in 1936 and soon after joined the British Interplanetary Society. After war broke out in Europe, he joined the Royal Air Force, where he worked in radar training and helped to develop "better systems for the RAF."[43]

The British Interplanetary Society (BIS) was founded in Liverpool in 1933 by Philip E. Cleator and is the oldest space advocacy organization in the world. Its aim is exclusively to support and promote astronautics and space exploration. It is situated on South Lambeth Road near Vauxhall Station, not far from the Secret Intelligence Service building. The BIS—by gathering together a number of writers and administrative talents—provided "a sudden violent motivation" to the world of British Science Fiction.[44]

In The *Challenge of the Spaceship*, Clarke wrote: "I have tried to show that the future development of mankind, on the spiritual no less than the material plane, is bound up with the conquest of space" (p. 21).

> Interplanetary travel is now the only form of "conquest and empire" compatible with civilization. Without it, the human mind, compelled to circle forever in its planetary goldfish bowl, must eventually stagnate ... Few things will do more to accelerate that evolution than the conquest of space. It is not easy to see how the more extreme forms of nationalism can long survive when men begin to see the Earth in its true perspective as a single small globe among the stars.[45]

The hidden function of movies as propaganda is a secret that has, for the most part, been hiding in plain sight. Nor do we have to look far to see that the tradition of science fiction space fantasy movies as cultural indoctrination continues to this day, for example, in the work of Kubrick "heir," Christopher Nolan:

> The film *Interstellar* should be shown in school science lessons, a scientific journal has urged ... The director of *Interstellar*, Christopher Nolan, told BBC News that Dr Jackson's comments and the two journal publications were "very important" to him. "Right from the beginning we all really believed it's time to inspire another generation to really look outwards and to look to the stars again. We hoped that by dramatising science and making it something that could be entertaining for kids we might inspire some of the astronauts of tomorrow—that would be the ultimate goal of the project," he said.[46]

This sort of stuff doesn't really have to be kept (all that) secret, because, after all, they aren't promoting war or corporate expansionism. Right? (Wrong.) But whatever happened to a movie is just a movie? There *were* no good old days, just a good old daze we were kept in. To the Kubraphiles voluntarily lost in the Overlook maze, seeking breadcrumbs that lead them further in, none of this is new or especially relevant: Kubrick, they counter, was *aware* of making state propaganda but intelligent enough to *subvert* the powers-that-be (his backers, open and secret) by embedding *clues* in the film to alert the viewer.

At the risk of presenting a circular argument, is this much power and influence given to someone who plans to subvert the groups and institutions giving it to him? If you want to make a war movie in Hollywood and need access to the hardware, the Pentagon has full script approval. How much more so with space stuff?

How effective has *2001* been in inspiring interest in space travel, ET gods, and a human destiny "beyond the infinite," and how effective at exposing film as a tool for state propaganda? Which of these two memes (or memeplexes) is more dominant today?

2001 is remembered above all as a work of film artistry and transcendent vision. The "space propaganda" aspects are all but forgotten—insofar as they were ever noticed at all—along with the idea that the film is best appreciated on LSD. Like all "art" (effective cultural engineering), it has outlasted and transcended those contexts, while at the same time raising them up to a higher level.

By turning space conquest into a metaphor for the ultimate realization of human potential, Kubrick and Clarke's film gave the highest form of legitimization to the space program: they *spiritualized* it. That this was (as is clearly documented) part of a corporate agenda to boost the space colonization industry—i.e., had *nothing at all* to do with man's spiritual potential—has been overlooked, because the idea of space travel as a benign and positive goal for human beings to pursue, to this day, is almost entirely unquestioned.

Yet the reason it is unquestioned can be attributed, in no small part, to works like *2001*.

UNITED STATES INFORMATION AGENCY
WASHINGTON

CONFIDENTIAL

June 4, 1965

MEMORANDUM FOR: Mr. Eric Goldman
Special Consultant
to the President
The White House

A. Miss Conklin of my staff has collated the recommendations of the six film critics who offered their estimates of the most important American filmmakers.

Attached is a complete breakdown for your records and the following is a summary of the individuals principally mentioned.

1. Four men were named by all six critics:

   Elia Kazan
   George Stevens
   William Wyler
   Fred Zinnemann

2. Stanley Kubrick was mentioned by four of the six critics (one of these was in the "most promising" category).

3. Three men were mentioned by three of the critics: Stanley Kramer, Alfred Hitchcock and Billy Wilder.

4. It should be noted that John Huston was named by five of the six critics but he is no longer an American citizen and according to my understanding this would remove him from consideration.

CONFIDENTIAL

Determined to be an administrative marking
By 7h On 10-9-71

COPY LBJ LIBRARY

CONFIDENTIAL

- 2 -

Therefore, per our discussion, my office will proceed to contact Kazan, Stevens, Wyler, Zinnemann and Kubrick. They will be asked what scenes they believe would best demonstrate their work. We will ask for alternatives so that we maintain latitude.

To reach our desired total of six, one of the group including Kramer, Hitchcock and Wilder should be designated. Perhaps we can wait on this until we see how the other selected scenes shape up.

B. I have initiated explorations of the projection equipment rental and this should be finalized next week as soon as the room and the time for the film showings is designated. I mentioned to Barbara Lee Diamonstein the need for total darkness in the room which is to be used.

C. I gave you my thoughts regarding a host for this part of the day earlier on the phone.

I think in order to lend long-range value to this undertaking a commentary should be written and delivered by someone outside of the motion picture field. It should be someone whose words are likely to add an appraisal of the motion picture as an American art form which would have more influence than one offered by an individual whose principal interest is motion pictures.

My suggestions were two:

1. Russell Baker whom I know only slightly but who has written humorous pieces which indicate that he has seen many motion pictures. I know nothing about his public speaking abilities nor do I know if he has a strong feeling about the place of the film in the United States or about the filmmakers who have been selected by the critics.

CONFIDENTIAL

COPY LBJ LIBRARY

CONFIDENTIAL

- 3 -

2. Arthur Schlesinger, Jr. is, in my opinion, one of the most interesting writers on the subject of films. It is, of course, a sidelight with him but he has written interesting pieces in Harpers Magazine, Show Magazine, and served on the Jury of last year's international festival at Cannes. The fact that Arthur was a member of the previous Administration may be a drawback - I am certain Jack Valenti could give you a quick reading on that factor as it now stands. Arthur's virtue for this is that he has a sense of films as they relate to American life and history, and I am certain he is familiar with most of the films which are likely to be shown at the presentation.

I think an important factor here is that President Johnson has led the way in giving the motion picture the recognition it has previously lacked in American political life. (By its important inclusion in the Arts Bill, the President's Council on the Arts, etc.) It is, therefore, particularly important that the person who handles this part of the program be truly knowledgeable and articulate on the subject so that this recognition is clearly justified.

If neither of these possibilities work out let me know and I will give it further thought.

George Stevens, Jr.
Director
Motion Picture Service

CONFIDENTIAL

COPY LBJ LIBRARY

KUBARK: sinister associations

"The first manual, 'KUBARK Counterintelligence Interrogation,' dated July 1963, is the source of much of the material in the second manual. KUBARK was a U.S. Central Intelligence Agency cryptonym for the CIA itself. The cryptonym KUBARK appears in the title of a 1963 CIA document KUBARK Counterintelligence Interrogation which describes interrogation techniques, including, among other things, 'coercive counterintelligence interrogation of resistant sources.' This is the oldest manual, and describes the use of abusive techniques, as exemplified by two references to the use of electric shock, in addition to the use of threats and fear, sensory deprivation, and isolation."

—Wikipedia

Whether or not Kubrick knew of scenario-planning and NASA's space-promotion plan (he was a smart guy, so I would guess he did), we have documented evidence of such a program, combined with more than circumstantial evidence that *2001* was a, if not *the*, major example of its implementation. That Kubrick was short-listed for recruitment in a government program for the making of film propaganda is indicated by the memorandum (reproduced above) sent by George Stevens Jr. (the founder of the American Film Institute), on behalf of the United States Information Agency, on June 4, 1965.

The memo is addressed to Eric Goldman, Special Consultant to the President, at the White House (Goldman was also an author who wrote for Henry Luce's *Time* magazine, a CIA-backed corporation under Project Mockingbird). The memo is marked "CONFIDENTIAL" and lists eight directors selected by film critics as "the most important American filmmakers" to be considered for an unspecified project. The filmmakers are Elia Kazan, George Stevens, William Wyler, Fred Zinnemann, Stanley Kubrick, Stanley Kramer, Alfred Hitchcock, and Billy Wilder. (John Huston is mentioned but vetoed as being no longer an American citizen. Hitchcock became a US citizen in 1955.)

Kubrick is mentioned as being in the "most promising" category. "Therefore, per our discussion, my office will proceed to contact Kazan, Stevens, Wyler, Zinnemann and Kubrick. They will be asked what scenes they believe will best demonstrate their work." The memorandum ends with this:

President Johnson has led the way in giving the motion picture industry the recognition it has previously lacked in American political life. (By its important inclusion in the Arts Bill, the President's Council on the Arts, etc.) It is, therefore, particularly important that the person who handles this part of the program be truly knowledgeable and articulate on the subject so that this recognition is clearly justified.

What was the program in question? There is no historical record of this memorandum besides the document itself (which someone got hold of via the Freedom of Information Act), so we are left to speculate. Among the growing numbers of internet detectives who believe the Moon landing footage (though not necessarily the Moon landing) was faked, and that Kubrick had a hand in it (presumably while ostensibly working on *2001*), the document, while falling somewhat short of a smoking gun, is confirmation of this theory. What it really confirms is that Kubrick was contacted by the public relations (propaganda) branch of the US government in 1965 and, judging by other evidence, that he was recruited by them *in some capacity*. This means that, whatever secret program he was recruited into, *2001*, the film he began to make at the time of his recruitment, *was central to it*.

Does any of this make *2001 ipso facto* a work of propaganda? The answer depends on how fervently you believe in the power of individual vision, or genius, to transcend corporate, government, and institutional agendas *while appearing to serve them*. There is much romantic appeal in the idea that Kubrick was able, like David facing down Goliath, not only to take on the whole Hollywood system but The System Itself, the US government, military, intelligence, the whole caboodle, and sneak one past them. It's tempting to make a joke at this point about a Stargate I've got to sell you, but that might be too much like shooting astronauts floating in a tin can.

What's clear from all this (to me at least) is that *2001* was part of a large, semi-covert push by the US government toward *propagating the necessity and desirability of space colonization*; and that this ties into a still larger program (laid out in *Prisoner of Infinity*) that includes mind control, psychedelic drugs, alien abduction beliefs, and the New Age movement, among other things.

My own impression of *2001*, at least the last time I sat through it, is that the film is imbued with American religiosity around the idea of man-made progress and, yes, the *triumph of the will to power* (right down to the Strauss soundtrack). I find the film pompous and bloated, lacking subtlety, nuance, or emotional depth. The final sequence of passing through the stargate—key to the work as a whole—is a singularly unimpressive light-show that goes on for a very long time but amounts to not very much—at least if the viewer hasn't already invested heavily in the transcendental narrative (or taken LSD).

In many ways, the movie strikes me now, 60 years on, as an Onanistic fantasy of technological transcendence that works for audiences only by stripping the moviegoing experience to its barest (or purest) essentials, that of light and sound, cunningly and artistically assembled to create a trance state. In other words, it provides a certain kind of moviegoer with the experience that he (it is mostly men) most fervently desires to *have* at a movie: to be raptured out of our mundane lives into a fantasy that, at the same time (unlike a comparable movie such as *Close Encounters of the Third Kind*), has pretensions toward serious philosophical meaning. This allows the dreamer to tell himself that this is no escapist fantasy at all, but "the ultimate trip": an experience as real as reality itself, or more so (the Monolith is the movie screen, remember).

The flip-side of Arthur C. Clarke's third law is that anything that *looks* like magic—or spirituality—is just a form of technology that we aren't advanced enough to grok yet.

* * *

> "Perhaps our role on this planet is not to worship God, but to create Him."
>
> —Arthur C. Clarke

Perhaps we should ask, at this point, how exactly would we expect propaganda to work in the hands of a "film genius"? There might be many levels. To take Kubrick's previous work—the one that got him his *2001* gig—*Dr. Strangelove or: How I Learned to Stop Worrying and Love the Bomb*, the film was apparently intended, and definitely received, as a cautionary satire on the insanity of nuclear weapons and the scientific, governmental, and (especially) military minds behind them. But was that really the effect it achieved, or was there something subtler going on beneath the surface (with or without Kubrick's ken)?

What Pauline Kael wrote of the film (in her review of *Bonnie and Clyde*) is worth quoting at length:

> *Dr. Strangelove* opened a new movie era. It ridiculed *everything* and *everybody* it showed, but concealed its own liberal pieties, thus protecting itself from ridicule. [It] was clearly intended as a cautionary movie; it meant to jolt us awake to the dangers of the bomb by showing us the insanity of the course we were pursuing. But artists' warnings about war and the dangers of total annihilation never tell us how we are supposed to regain control, and *Dr. Strangelove*, chortling over madness, did not indicate any possibilities for sanity. It was experienced not as satire but as a confirmation of fears. Total laughter carried the day. A new generation enjoyed seeing the world as insane; they *literally* learned to stop worrying and love the bomb. Conceptually, we had already been living with the bomb; now the mass audience of the movies—which is the youth of America—grasped the idea that the threat of extinction can be used to devaluate everything, to turn it all into a joke. And the members of this audience do love the bomb; they love feeling that the worst has happened and the irrational are the sane, because there is the bomb as the proof that the rational are insane. They love the bomb because it intensifies their feelings of hopelessness and powerlessness and innocence … Far from being purged, the spectators are paralyzed, but they're still laughing … It is not war that has been laughed to scorn but the possibility of sane action.

To the extent Kael is right, it might be said that Kubrick's vision for the film backfired. But it could also be argued that at some level there was an intentional, alternate message embedded in the film, which is closer to the effect Kael describes. In a piece on the origins of Klaus Schwab's Word Economic Forum (the visibly driving force behind "the Great Reset" in Europe in 2023), Johnny Vedmore traces the origins of the WEF back to the CIA, Henry Kissinger, and Herman Khan, among others. Kahn and Kissinger have both been suggested as inspirations for the *Dr. Strangelove* character, and in passing Vedmore mentions Kahn's alleged friendship with Kubrick. Vedmore also implies the film was consistent with, if not integral to, ongoing psychological operations with which these individuals and agencies were involved:

The ruling Establishment would discover that marrying the drama of conflict scenarios with media such as film would be extremely useful, almost akin to creating self-propagating propaganda in some cases. Films like Stanley Kubrick's *Dr Strangelove* were fantastic vehicles for people to understand the absurdity of thermonuclear disaster scenario planning. If people perceive you as an all-powerful evil villain then you may not gain the support of the common man, but you will gain the attention from those who seek power and wealth, or, how Klaus Schwab would refer to them, the "stakeholders" in society. This is very important to understand—the projection of extreme wealth and power will attract and bring the "stakeholders" of society to the World Economic Forum's table.[47]

A similar lens can also be brought to *2001*. The most superficial reading of the film would be the first target audience layer, for whom the notion that space travel—fired by man's innate drive to conquer—leads to transcendence. We have already covered the evidence that NASA backed the film for exactly these reasons, and *2001*'s influence on both filmmakers and technological developers ("rocket scientists") can hardly be overestimated. Implicit in this message is the seed of the idea that, somehow, not even despite but *because* of our inherent brutality to one another, our destiny as human beings lies in the stars. This belief is a scientistic equivalent of the religious aspiring for Heaven.

The next target audience layer is made up of less literal-minded viewers, for whom the film is a parable about transcending spacetime and entering into hyper-dimensional consciousness, and/or reunion with an infinite space God (re-immersion in the mother's psyche, for the Freudians). For these people, it might confirm a belief (for example) that the "shamanic" use of "entheogens" is a legitimate means to rediscover the star child of our souls.

From here, we can continue going ever deeper into ever subtler readings of the film, all of which refer back to Kubrick's creative genius, and none to NASA's covert corporate propaganda campaign. The one thing that seems fundamental to all readings of the film is the idea of a *linear progression from a primitive state to demigod status*, by whatever means; in other words, *human progress*.

2001's primary function is as a high-culture delivery device for scientism, which both gravitates around and is powered by the meme of "God-as-Extra-Terrestrial," i.e., the materiality of the divine. This meme is a populist one (witness von Daniken books and the Discovery Channel's "ancient astronauts") that is "unscientific" and so had to come in by the back door of the arts. High-culture meets low-culture in the body and work of Stanley Kubrick, most especially *2001*, which allows scientific-minded folk to hang out on Hollywood Blvd, and feel rightly represented, while giving the general populace (most specifically stoner kids) the feeling of hobnobbing with the elites, getting to enjoy a piece of sensationalist entertainment that has all the earmarks of "art," and all the weight of legitimate "science" behind it.

Just because Kubrick is showing the emptiness, and even pathology, of technology doesn't mean he isn't celebrating it—just as he went on to celebrate the freedom of psychopathy in *A Clockwork Orange*. The two films even complement one another, like dark and light, in propagating the notion that, through the will to power, dissociated as it may be, true transcendence will eventually occur.

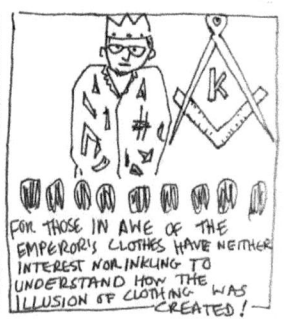

CHAPTER 5

Clockwork conspiracy theories

> "The criminal and the solider have the virtue of being *for* something or *against* something in a world where many people have learned to accept gray nothingness, to strike an unreal series of poses in order to be considered 'normal' or 'average.' It's difficult to say who is engaged in the greater conspiracy—the criminal, the soldier, or us."
> —Stanley Kubrick

Secret knowledge puts those close to you at risk. It's a heavy burden for anyone to carry, much less for an artist whose creative process supposedly hinges on freedom of expression. Exploring the unconscious and expressing it really means exploring the unconscious *by* expressing it. (What's unconscious can only be discovered after it's already expressed, at least in part.) Yet this would be an unacceptable risk for anyone whose survival—and continued success—depends on keeping a tight lid on things. Is this why Kubrick's movies seem empty of unconscious matter? A director presides over a series of accidents, so said Orson Welles (who admired Kubrick). Yet was ever a director less accident-friendly or more tightly controlled than Kubrick?

The Kubrick mystery, like the mystery of life, can't be explained away by any one theory. The element of a huge, political secret that Kubrick was obliged to keep, however, seems to me an essential, even indispensable, element in understanding Kubrick's "game"—or at least, the level at which he was playing it.

Kubrick began his career filming boxing matches in New York—i.e., in close proximity to the Mob. He found an independently wealthy backer, James B. Harris, for his third film and never had to raise money for his movies after that, or even work for a studio in the usual sense (with the exception of *Spartacus*). He remains a historical anomaly from that time, arriving as he did over a decade ahead of the independent film movement (Godard, Cassavetes, and others made films in the 1960s, but Kubrick led the way). Kubrick was friends with Arthur C. Clark and John Le Carré, both of whom had links to elite factions of government and/or the intelligence community. In the 1970s, according to his assistant Tony Frewin, Kubrick created a fake film company as a front so he could work on his films in the earliest stages (pre-pre-production) under a cloak of absolute secrecy. This is not how filmmakers generally operate, but it *is* how intelligence agents work.

How does an artist rise to the ranks of the elite? Probably not at all, but that the elite know how to recruit, train, and position artists to further their own social goals would seem a logical deduction. And if you want to join an organized crime ring, you first have to commit a crime, because only then can you be trusted.

So what was Kubrick's first "kill"?

Some facts about Stanley

> "Stanley is like a vampire of people's brains. He draws out whatever he thinks anybody knows. He just goes on and on in that rather flat voice to get out what people know."
> —Adrienne Corri

What follows are some (to me) intriguing tidbits that showed up in the reading of John Baxter's *Stanley Kubrick*. For the most part, in the interests of brevity and concision, I will simply list them without commentary.

Kubrick was born June 26, 1928, in the Bronx, New York. During the period he grew up in:

> There was much talk of technocracy—government by scientists. "What seems inevitable in the future," H.G. Wells had said in 1899, "is the rule by an aristocracy of organizers, men who manage railroads and similar vast enterprises." Wells could not have cared for the reality, of government controlled by soundbites and headed by actors and TV executives, and nor did Kubrick, whose conviction that life can, and should, be run on rational, even mechanical lines took root early. If that meant he would have to live alone in his tower, like John Masteran, the administrator king of Fritz Lang's *Metropolis*, it was a price he was ready to pay.
>
> (Baxter, p. 19)

Between 1942 and 1945 (aged 14 to 17), Kubrick attended William Howard Taft High School in the Bronx, which Baxter describes as "closer to a prison than a school" (p. 23).

The famous photo that gave Kubrick his break in the photography business was of a sad-faced news vendor next to a copy of the *Daily Mirror* with the headline, "FDR is Dead." This snapshot got him work at *Look* magazine in 1946, at age 18. "Kubrick told everyone it was a lucky shot … To Walter Trueman, however, he confessed he'd sweated blood persuading the old man to look appropriately dejected—an early example of his taxing method with actors" (ibid., p 27). On becoming a member of *Look* staff, Kubrick's friend Alex Singer reported: "Stanley had very carefully made that possible. He'd gone through a very deliberate set of plans to get there" (ibid., p. 29).

Kubrick used some of the money he earned at *Look* to take flying lessons, and in 1947 he was issued with a pilot's certificate. His early New York friends included Faith Hubley, Bert Stern, and celebrated photographer Diane Arbus, "who often took Kubrick to Saturday night charades parties in the Village."

Kubrick worked in the early 1950s on miscellaneous television and "state department trivia." His second documentary was about a New Mexican priest, Father Fred Stadtmueller. In 1952, he made a documentary about the World Assembly of Youth, "an initiative that was to have its pay-off in JFK's Peace Corps" (ibid., p. 51). His first feature came out in 1953.

Three years earlier, at age 21, Kubrick met Richard de Rochemont. De Rochement was the younger brother of Louis de Rochement, creator of the famous *March of Time* series (cinema newsreels, as parodied by Orson Welles in *Citizen Kane*). Richard de Rochemont worked as a producer on that series and took over as executive producer in 1943. A Harvard graduate and documentary filmmaker, he was associated with General Charles du Gaulle during World War II and wrote reportage for Henry Luce's *Life* magazine (Operation Mockingbird). Kubrick biographer Vincent LoBrutto writes that Richard de Rochemont "was responsible for France's rallying around De Gaulle and against the Vichy government" and that he was "highly decorated with honors in the country of his French Huguenot family" (p. 77). Perhaps no surprise, then, to learn that the older Louis

> was trained by British Intelligence in the early 1920s at the Massachusetts Institute of Technology to pioneer naval photography and motion picture reconnaissance. Dwight D. Eisenhower personally recruited him for the position of secretary of the Navy as World War II broke out. He declined the invitation, requesting instead to serve the country by "bringing the war to the American people."[48]

Louis also produced *Animal Farm*, funded by the CIA under Operation Mockingbird, and "mediated the relationship between the CIA's E. Howard Hunt and Sonia Blair, [George Orwell's] widow."[49]

According to LoBrutto, it was via Richard de Rochemont's support—financial and otherwise—that Kubrick's first film, *Fear and Desire*, was completed, released, and reviewed, thereby establishing Kubrick as an up-and-coming independent New York filmmaker. De Rochemont "was Kubrick's benefactor, boss, and father figure. Kubrick once told Dick's wife, Jane, 'You know we're really Dick's children'" (p. 87). The de Rochemont power family—complete with *direct links* to British Intelligence, the CIA, and Operation Mockingbird—put Stanley on the map.

Flashback: in the early 40s, the filmmaker Luis Buñuel was also in New York, where he joined a committee to educate members of the US government on the effectiveness of film as a medium of propaganda. Buñuel was hired to produce a shortened version of Leni Riefenstahl's *Triumph of the Will* as a demonstration project. Buñuel stayed at the Museum of Modern Art (a known CIA front according to Saunders' *Cultural Cold War*) to work for the Office of the Coordinator of Inter-American Affairs (OCIAA) as part of a production team that would gather, review, and edit films intended as anti-fascist propaganda, to be distributed in Latin America by American embassies.

Returning to 1953: *Fear and Desire*, doubled with Buñuel's *El Bruto*. Flash-forward to 1971–1972: Buñuel was a vocal admirer of *Clockwork Orange*, whom Kubrick quoted when defending the film. One thing Buñuel knew about, evidently, was propaganda. *Fear and Desire* was reviewed by most of the major press "for patriotic reasons if no other" (Baxter, p. 55). Apparently, Kubrick also knew a few tricks.

Learning from The Master

> "The 'chess mind' is one that can retain thousands of games, and consider and reject hundreds of alternatives before choosing the best move for a particular situation."
> —Stanley Kubrick

As is well-known, Kubrick was an avid chess player.

> The NY chess scene encouraged those aspects of Kubrick's character which psychologists call "passive/aggressive." He had developed, like many men who shared this personality defect—T.E. Lawrence, Howard Hughes—the tendency ... of "backing into the limelight." There was a narcissism in Kubrick's shyness, a tendency to choose the act of self-effacement which would most stridently draw attention to itself.
> (Baxter, p. 33)

Kubrick learned from a street chess player, "The Master"

> a battery of psychological games that he used throughout his filmmaking career to keep both opponents and friends off balance. The urgent, nocturnal summons, the lawyer's letter appearing out of the blue, the sudden phone call revealing his unexpected possession of information, the abrupt change of mood during filming, or the demand for some enigmatic object or obscure alteration to the script, set or performance: these became tools of Kubrick's trade.
> (Baxter, p. 42)

Kubrick's pal Alex Singer was drafted in 1953 and posted at US Army's Signal Corps Photographic Center in Paramount's old studios in Astoria, Long Island. Also posted there was James B. Harris, Kubrick's future producer. Harris's father was a "wealthy New York insurance broker [who had] funded some film distribution deals" (ibid., p. 42). Before he went into business with Harris, however, Kubrick made his second feature, *Killer's Kiss*, in 1955. He was 26 years old and—according to the lore—funded the movie with $40,000 borrowed from his uncle, who owned a drug store in New York. The female star of *Killer's Kiss* was Irene Kane, who commented that Kubrick is "all for sex and sadism" (ibid., p. 63). Baxter concurs: "It would appear from his films that Kubrick is excited by the image of helpless and sexually threatened women" (ibid., p. 66).

Following the release of *Killer's Kiss*, James B. Harris and Kubrick formed a partnership, though they "never had any agreement in writing between [them]" (ibid., pp. 70–71). Their first film was the downbeat heist drama *The Killing*. *The Killing* was released in May of 1956; in June of the same year, *Time* magazine ran an article titled "The New Pictures" that stated: "At twenty-seven, writer-director Stanley Kubrick, in his third full-length picture, has shown more audacity with dialogue and camera than Hollywood has seen since the obstreperous Orson Welles went riding out of town on an exhibitor's poll." As LoBrutto describes this publicity *coup*: "The ever-elusive King-of-Hollywood-hill scepter was now in Stanley Kubrick's hands" (p. 126)—with his first semi-widespread release! Someone might have added, "courtesy of Luce's *Time-Life* and the CIA's Operation Mockingbird."

When Kubrick went to Los Angeles for the film, he met Curtis Harrington and Gavin Lambert, who "introduced him to what they regarded as its secret delights, like the home of so-called 'male witch' Samson DeBrier on Barton Avenue in Hollywood, a mecca for every oddball in the city." This included Ivor Stravinsky, James Dean, and Kenneth Anger, who shot *Inauguration of the Pleasure Dome* there. According to Baxter, DeBrier's home may have been "the model for Quilty's decaying mansion in *Lolita*" (ibid., p. 78). Anger was a Crowleyite whose involvement with the darker aspects of occultism—and ties to groups like the Process Church, the Manson family, and intelligence programs such as MKULTRA—are as striking as his influence on major filmmakers such as Kubrick, Scorsese, and David Lynch.

Following *The Killing*, Kubrick had his first prestige hit with *Paths of Glory*, which put him into a brief partnership with Kirk Douglas. Between *Paths of Glory* and *Spartacus*, Kubrick got embroiled in the Marlon Brando project *One-Eyed Jacks*. Baxter notes that "Kubrick was being put through elaborate tests of *machismo* and expertise, not unlike those which he would impose on his own collaborators in later years. It was from Brando that he learned them" (ibid., p. 117).

(Before Kubrick came aboard the project, Sam Peckinpah was fired as scriptwriter. Later, Peckinpah said of the experience, "Brando taught me to hate." Yet, according to Baxter's account, it was *Kubrick* who disliked Peckinpah's script and insisted Brando have him replaced! So who taught whom to hate, and who learned the macho ways of Hollywood skullduggery from whom? Perhaps Peckinpah blamed Brando for diplomatic reasons, and to avoid dissing a fellow director who would go on to dwarf his own "legendary" status—since that would only sound like sour grapes?)

For the making of *2001*, Kubrick's assistant Andrew Birkin "bribed park rangers, laid on a midnight truck convoy, cut down half a dozen [strictly protected] trees" in order to stick the coveted "two-hundred-year-old kookabong tree" in a shot that never made it into the finished cut (Baxter, p. 220).

A number of people working on *2001* suffered various forms of nervous breakdown. As assistant editor David de Wilde put it, "Stanley had that effect on people. I mean, how many people had nervous breakdowns on the film? Have you worked that out? A lot of people. Stanley used to put the fear of God into people, without doing anything" (Benson, p. 355).

According to Arthur C. Clarke (quoted by Baxter, p. 206): "Stanley was in some danger of believing in flying saucers. I felt I had arrived just in time to save him from this gruesome fate." On *2001*, Kubrick became convinced that art department members "spent most of their time chatting and drinking tea [and] briefly contemplated setting up hidden TV surveillance cameras to spy on them, until others on the unit more acquainted with British union rules advised him that even to contemplate such a move would result in an immediate strike" (ibid., p. 217). Stanley's intelligence training, showing itself again?

The Sci-Fi novelist Clancy Sigal visited the *2001* set and reported:

> Everyone on this film I've met is tremendously responsible; all work and exist as if under the shadow of some great, looming bomb. It causes publicity people to talk like presidential candidates, assistant directors to walk like Trappist monks and the art and science people involved to wear the expression of bemused,

> satisfied contentment that I have always associated with drier and more corporate enterprises, such as NASA and General Motors.
>
> (Ibid., p. 222)

HAL's capabilities, like all the technology in *2001*, were based on the speculation of respected scientists, including Marvin Minsky, Director of the MIT Computer Science and Artificial Intelligence Laboratory, an adviser on the film set.[50] In 2019, Minsky was accused by a victim of billionaire Jeffrey Epstein, who claimed she was forced to have sex with him.[51]

For Leonard Rosenman, a musician who worked on *Barry Lyndon*, Kubrick is "brilliant but he reduces everyone to slaves" (ibid., p. 292). On Kubrick's militaristic directing tactics, Baxter writes:

> Both [Napoleon and Kubrick] kept a mental roster of the people on their personal staff, and subtly rotated them in and out of favor. A man praised one week would find himself progressively less valued, until even his most energetic efforts were rewarded with nothing but icy stares. Soon after, however, he would be elevated abruptly to a favored position again. The system kept subordinates subtly off-balance, and too busy competing for their leader's favor to waste time or intrigue against him.
>
> (Ibid., p. 236)

It's interesting to note that, while he made his name with a powerful anti-war statement (*Paths of Glory*), Kubrick never attempted to disguise his predilection for warfare: "Napoleonic battles are so beautiful, like vast lethal ballets ... They all have an aesthetic brilliance that doesn't require a military mind to appreciate ... It's almost like a great piece of music or the purity of a mathematical formula" (ibid., p. 237).

Are Kubrick's choices simply a case of knowing what sort of propaganda was in demand at any given time for furthering his mission? Next up—now the counterculture had crashed and burned, and acid was just a bad flashback—was a bit of the old ultra-violence. As Baxter notes (p. 243): "Full frontal nudity, profanity, sacrilege and political protest were the common currency of the new American cinema. Kubrick, at forty, looked like a dinosaur. The sense that he was out of date, a back number, stung. If he couldn't make 'Napoleon,' he could make a youth film that would outrage the best of them."

Agent Orange

"A director is a kind of idea and tastes machine."
—Stanley Kubrick

Earlier I referred to "My brush with the porno underworld." The event happened on one of my adolescent movie-stalking jaunts from Yorkshire to London, maybe the same trip I first saw *Dirty Harry* or *Texas Chainsaw Massacre* or *Taxi Driver*. I was both industrious and imaginative, and sought the forbidden fruit in what was the closest thing to an underworld I could find: the porn district of Soho. That would have been a new experience for me, because my taste in auto-erotic stimulation aids was mostly met by video nasties (along with the occasional ultra-soft-core *Playboy* video and raunchy comedies like *Kentucky Fried Movie*).

For my first ever excursion onto the porn circuit, I was emboldened—relatively freed from shame or furtive apprehension—by the knowledge that I was on a quest for art and not smut, albeit art that had been wrongfully forbidden by the heathens of moral prudery. Or so I thought—that it was Kubrick's own censure that led me into this seamy underworld is something I was unaware of back then, though it is perhaps the most telling irony of the tale.

Since I was an innocent among thieves, I was an easy mark for the first rogue I came across—or the first porno shopkeeper. This one listened to my query (that I was looking for the banned Kubrick masterpiece), nodded his head and, to my growing excitement, said he did indeed have a pirate copy "in the back." He warned me that I couldn't tell anyone where I had got it (verisimilitude), to which I eagerly complied. He withdrew out of sight to return moments later with a blank cassette, which he put inside a brown paper bag. He named a price (£20?) and I paid it without hesitation. (Whatever I could have afforded is what I would have agreed to.)

In retrospect, this was the original Kubrick disappointment, maybe even the blueprint. Not (this time) that *A Clockwork Orange* was a grossly overrated movie, but that this was not an *orange* at all (closer to an apple): I had bought a softcore porno movie, something that was, even at the best of times but never more so than now, of little interest to me. If memory serves, it was an oriental *Emmanuelle* movie. I don't think I even watched it.

Nor did it end there. I went back to the shop on my next trip to London, taking the useless cassette with me. I have a dim memory of the man's excuse—both brilliant and feeble at the same time—that he had to be sure he could *trust* me before he gave me the real thing! He then (I believe) went into the back and we reenacted *the exact same steps as before*, as once again he handed me the phony merchandise, and, once again, desire overrode common sense, and I took it. Fool me once, shame on you. Fool me twice, etc.

Is this early evidence of my induction into the Kubrick con? I let the jury decide.

A clean-minded pornographer

> "Is there anything sadder—and ultimately more repellant—than a clean-minded pornographer?"
>
> —Pauline Kael, "Stanley Strangelove"

Writing about the rape with which Kubrick opens *A Clockwork Orange*, Kael writes, "That girl is stripped for our benefit; it's the purest exploitation." In fact, Kubrick changed the scene from the book by replacing a 13-year-old victim with a big-breasted woman, and it is certainly shot for erotic appeal and not for horror's sake. I speak with authority: when I finally got my own copy of the film (the same week I moved to New York, at age 20), it was this sequence that provided me with fodder for auto-erotic stimulation.

Kubrick went to great pains to find the right—sufficiently stimulating—breasts, too. Adrienne Corri (who plays the second rape victim in the film) recalls: "The casting director told me, 'Adrienne, he's asking practically every actress in London to go into this little office with a hidden video camera and take off their blouse and bra so he can look at their tits ...' Stanley asked me to audition semi-nude for the role, but I refused. 'But suppose we don't like the tits, Corri?'" (Baxter, p. 251). This was the same Kubrick, mind, who flirted with the idea of making "Hollywood's first big-budget porn feature" (ibid, p. 179). Is there anything sadder?

Kael also points out how Kubrick altered the novel, in both detail and essence, to make Alex the hero of the film, not just by casting McDowell and making his the only likable performance in the film, but by leaving out the character's more unsavory habits, such as running over small animals and raping 10-year-old girls. The novel's author, Anthony Burgess, certainly had cause for complaint. In his autobiography, he "painted himself as the victim of a manipulative [Jimmy] Savile and an even more Machiavellian Kubrick" (ibid., p. 271).

Why the juxtaposition of Kubrick with the notorious DJ and child rapist Jimmy Savile? Burgess was on a talk show about the film, hosted by Savile. Savile, along with Kubrick, set Burgess up to take the rap for the film's incitement of violence—despite the fact that it was the film, not the book, that glorified Alex and turned ultra-violence into a way of "sucking up to the thugs in the audience." If Burgess didn't protest more than he did, or denounce the film, the reason is probably that he *was* complicit from the start.

As reported by Paul Gallagher in "Anthony Burgess and The Top Secret Code in *A Clockwork Orange*,"[52] Burgess biographer Roger Lewis was told by a source in British Intelligence that *A Clockwork Orange*

> was about the mind-control experimentation conducted by Dr. Ewen Cameron at the Allen Memorial Institute in Montreal, between 1957 and 1963, and the Remote Neural Monitoring facility that operated out of Fort George Meade. The CIA were funding controversial research programmes into electronic brain stimulation. They induced exhaustion and nightmares in patients; they put hoods or cones over people's heads to broadcast voices directly into their brains; they irradiated the auditory cortex or inner ear. When patients had their own speech played back to them, incessantly, they went insane. There was a misuse of civilians in these covert operations, and intelligence on these devices remains classified.

Lewis believed that Burgess "had been a low-grade collector of intelligence data (or ground observer) in the Far East" for the British and that, on his return to England, he found himself in a world of spy scandals (Guy Burgess, Philby, and Maclean) and double agents (George Blake), which led American intelligence to question its relationship with British Intelligence. Burgess was assigned to *front a novel* that would "lift the corner of the carpet and put into his novel classified material about the (then) new-fangled conditioning experiments and aversion therapies being devised to reform criminals—experiments which had wider implications for the concept of social engineering."[53]

84   THE KUBRICKON

Lewis claims there is *a secret message* hidden in Burgess' text, and that "the capitalised lines on page twenty-nine of *A Clockwork Orange* give the HQ location of the psychotronic warfare technology"—referring to a section in the book that describes the college pennants on Alex's wall, each of these "being like remembrances of my corrective school life since I was eleven, O my dear brothers …"

> The spy explained to Lewis that if he looked at a map of America, then he would see that Utah, Colorado, Arizona and New Mexico are the only states with a right-angled four-corner conjunction ("4 … COR"), and that there is a military reservation to the "SOUTH." This reservation runs north into New Mexico, and is situated around the "METRO"-politan area of El Paso. This is where the training school ("SKOL") is situated. At the time of the book's publication (1962), the Navy ("BLUE DIVISION") were in charge of this operation: Analysing, isolating and interfering with the "ALPHA" wavelengths of the human collective unconsciousness was part of the set-up. The name of the establishment is Fort Bliss. The word bliss appears on page twenty-nine of Burgess's novel no less than six times.

Lewis believes that espionage made Burgess rich, and was the "dark secret haunting him" to the end.

* * *

> "Never, ever go near power. Don't become friends with anyone who has real power. It's dangerous."
> —Kubrick, quoted by Christiane Kubrick, "After Stanley Kubrick"

None of this was even remotely on my mind when I finally managed to see the movie (I still haven't read the book) in some Parisian repertoire theater in 1982. I am sure I was impressed by the movie—after all that build-up I would have convinced myself to be—but not so much that it made it onto my top ten list. By the time I wrote about it in 1997–1998, I would have seen it half a dozen times and come to dislike it quite intensely. Even then, I had no clue as to the shadowy origins. Well, not exactly no clue, but no evidence. I was still just writing about movies then, slipping in a morsel of paranoid awareness wherever I could, in the hope it would be seen as ironic and playful, as for example, when I wrote: "The film seems to have been made by the behavior-modification boys at MKULTRA." What's in a quip? Even at that time, I am fairly sure I believed it.

Here are some of the other things I wrote:

> Kubrick's films assume a calculated indifference to pain, or to passion (and therefore to poetry also)—they are about absence of feeling, which is about as lousy a subject as any so-called artist can possibly alight on ... *A Clockwork Orange* gives us an overdose of irony; and yet the final resolution, by somehow reconciling and realizing all the collective ironies into a single, sick joke, seems to be the only honest, unambiguous moment in the film.

Reading this now, it seems to me that Alex is, in many ways, the quintessential Kubrick hero—prior to Jack Torrance at least—in his "calculated indifference to pain"—he is the psychopath who knows himself (and shows himself) only through violence. All other Kubrick leads, from *Dr. Strangelove* on, are passive, deranged, or both. By comparison, Alex seems relatively individualized. The tragedy of the film—and the repellant sadness of Kubrick, the clean-minded porn merchant—is that he is also the closest a Kubrick hero comes to *passion*. That Alex fully embraces his thuggish nature at the film's climax seems to be the only redemption Kubrick can imagine for his creations. Short of a computer-generated star child, it is back to the ape or bust. Yet (as I wrote in 1998),

> Alex's demons are not the primal demons of the natural man—atavistic rage let loose in a moment of crisis—they are rather technological, social demons, bred and indoctrinated into him by a machinelike system that has no respect for persons ... Kubrick is "interested"—if that's the word—in lack of soul, and all that that implies: vacuity, hollowness, despair, of a kind, but a despair that comes not from feeling too much, but from feeling nothing at all. Alex isn't evil, he's merely indifferent (and, as Kubrick presents him, irresponsible). He finds it so hard to feel anything at all that the only thing that really satisfies him, that makes him feel alive, is ultra-violence—the ultimate "sensation." Judging by this film at least, Kubrick seems to think about the same of his audience. The film seems to have been made by the behavior-modification

> boys at MKULTRA: it's designed to overwhelm us, to seduce us, and to satiate us, to leave us no room for honest reactions. Far from turning us off to the violence it shows us, it is actually turning us on to it, as the only real sensation we can get from the movie.

This is more or less what Kael wrote in her review, and many of my responses were no doubt "modified" by the countless times I read it, both before and after seeing the film (the last time being this afternoon). From *The Blood Poets*:

> Kubrick panders to our lack of sensitivity and thereby increases it. The artificiality of the sets, the clunking sparseness of the direction, the gibbering histrionics of the performers, the ugliness of the lighting, all combine to make the film so harrowing an experience (aesthetically not morally) that the scenes of giddy brutality come, perversely, as a kind of relief: they're the only time the characters—and the director—seem to come to life … Kubrick savors what he is supposed to be condemning, and no one seems to notice that his film is wholly devoid of either moral depth or simple human compassion (it's not that these things are necessary to justify art; they're necessary to *make* art).

Like Kael, expressions of moral concern were few and far between in my film writings, or anywhere. Yet, as with Kael, Kubrick seemed to bring that side out of me in full force. (Kael championed film violence most of the time, but when it came to *Orange*—and Clint Eastwood—she fully and firmly *balked*.) What neither of us addressed directly was how the crux of the problem may have related to Kubrick's use of film as a clinical medium for perception management, also known as propaganda. *Orange* has all the earmarks of a work designed by committee but, like Burgess' novel, fronted by a single, culturally positioned individual. In other words,

> *Clockwork Orange* has the thematic basis for a great, angry, crazy, surrealist comedy along the lines of a '70s *Manchurian Candidate*, and it may be this latent potential more than anything that the critics responded to. But Kubrick turns everything on its head, so that we laugh when we should be appalled, and feel queasy when we would be better off laughing. The perversity he shows for reducing

the material to his own unfathomable ends is very nearly on a par with that of the state itself—he might even be working for it, seeing as he never actually exposes it for what it is. The film is a travesty, and I suspect that's largely why it is considered a classic. It presents us with a puzzling dilemma all right, and in the most direct and troublesome fashion—the film itself is part of the problem.

Here I did seem to be fully aware of what I wanted to say, if not quite willing to say it in anything but "figurative" terms: "very nearly," "might even," and so on. The notion that Kubrick might be, like Buñuel before him, a state-hired official working in a superficially unofficial capacity had not, at that time, dawned on me.

> Kubrick tells us that Alex's natural brutality is the only thing that keeps him human, that separates him from the machine, yet all the while he's secretly despising the animal, and glorifying "the beast." Kubrick's alliance, here as elsewhere, is clearly with the machine, and that's what makes his films almost impossible to get a handle on—*they don't have a human perspective* ... By presenting a world in which the choice is between animal savagery and mechanical obedience—and by keeping the two alternatives at odds—Kubrick denies any possibility of the creative or spiritual impulses in man to emerge; he dismisses them, with a shake of his hairy, academic head, as so much chimera. By denying us the natural and indispensable refuge of "soul," he completes and rests his case, all right, but he also rejects any gifts he might once have had. A man without potential for savagery may make a poor animal indeed, but an artist without soul is nothing at all—he's like a mechanical watchdog: a clockwork clockmaker.

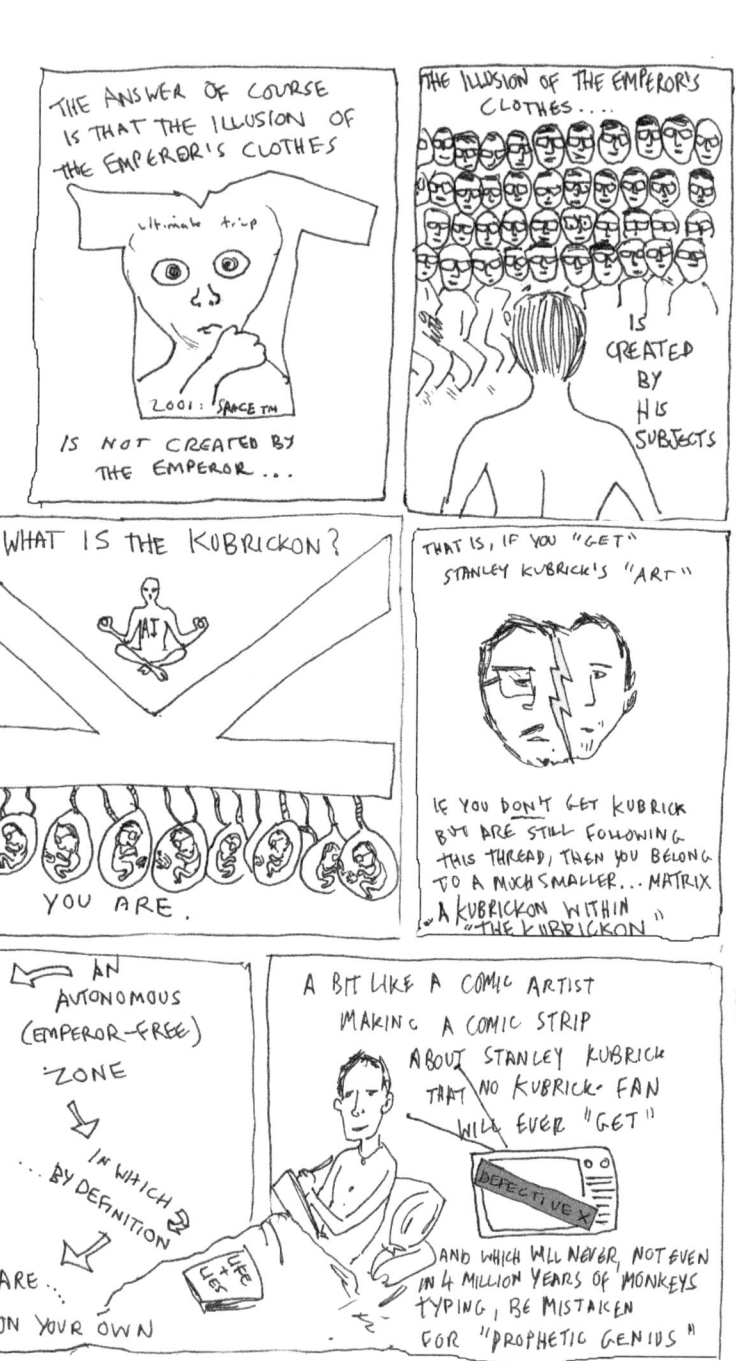

CHAPTER 6

The lost language of the body

"Before there was an internet, there was Stanley Kubrick."
—Christiane Kubrick

Kubrick, DARPA, Simulmatics

"This danger can be stated in the form of a simple equation, which I think might be the defining equation of life in the twenty-first century: B x C x D = AHH! Which means? Biological knowledge multiplied by computing power multiplied by data equals the ability to hack humans ... If you know enough biology and have enough computing power and data, you can hack my body and my brain and my life, and you can understand me better than I understand myself. You can know my personality type, my political views, my sexual preferences, my mental weaknesses, my deepest fears and hopes. You know more about me than I know about myself. And you can do that not just to me, but to everyone. A system that understands us better than we understand ourselves can predict our feelings and decisions, can manipulate our feelings and decisions, and can ultimately make decisions for us. [S]oon at least some corporations and governments will be able to systematically hack all the people. We humans should get used to the idea that we are no longer mysterious souls—we are now hackable animals."

—WEF member Dr. Yuval Noah Harari

What follows is a very brief history of the internet, with reference primarily to Steve Snider's opus-in-progress, *The Secret History of Conspiratainment*.

By the early 1960s, the Pentagon was spending nearly $15 million annually on psychology, much of it geared toward behavioral science. In 1967 alone, "$40 million was earmarked for social research, much of it related to psychology and behavioral science. And at the forefront of these efforts by then was ARPA." ARPA stands for Advanced Research Projects Agency; later the D of DARPA was added, for Defense. Central to ARPA was the development of computer technology and its appliance for counterinsurgency in military strategy. Several projects (ComCom, Camelot, Cambridge) were equally devoted to the science of predicting human behavior.

ARPA's Behavioral Science Program was run by computer scientist and trained psychologist J. C. R. "Lick" Licklider, also credited as the "visionary" behind the ARPANet, i.e., the original, military-designated internet. Licklider has been described as one of the "earliest and most ardent advocates" of Canadian neuroscientist Donald Hebb, a leading player behind MKULTRA. As Snider writes,

> The role behavioral science played in both the Cambridge/Camelot projects and the later Cambridge Analytica debacle is not a coincidence. Behavioral science was an abomination that began to take form during the 1950s. Partial inspiration came from the discipline of radical behaviorism, developed by Harvard psychiatrist B.F. Skinner. Skinner and his acolytes reduced human beings to an organism that could be managed via proper stimuli. All that was needed was enough experimentation and data to refine this process.

Involved in all of these projects was a corporation known as Simulmatics, which was "the brainchild of a New York ad man named Edward Greenfield." Greenfield's stated goal was "a political consulting firm that used computers to model and predict election results."

Among those he recruited (starting at the Ford Foundation's Center for Advanced Study in the Behavioral Sciences, located at Stanford University) was Eugene Burdick, co-author (with William J. Lederer) of *The Ugly American* and *Fail-Safe* (with Harvey Wheeler). After some early involvement, Burdick turned down a long-term position at Simulmatics; *The Ugly American* was a bestseller, so he was financially stable, and Burdick considered the company "dangerous." He was no stranger to danger, either: a character in *The Ugly American*—Col. Edwin Barnum Hillendale—was based on General Edward Lansdale, the infamous—see *16 Maps of Hell*—counterinsurgency specialist and leading player in the development of psychological warfare in the Philippines and South Vietnam. A number of Landsdale's protégés were also involved in Simulmatics;[54] according to Snider, Simulmatics even participated in the notorious (and terrorist) Phoenix Program.

This is from a 2020 *New Yorker* piece by Jill Lepore:

> Simulmatics ... built a very early version of the machine in which humanity would find itself trapped in the early twenty-first century, a machine that applies the science of psychological warfare to the affairs of ordinary life, a machine that manipulates opinion, exploits attention, commodifies information, divides voters, atomizes communities, alienates individuals, and undermines democracy. Facebook, Palantir, Cambridge Analytica, Amazon, the Internet Research Agency, Google: these are, every one, the children of Simulmatics. "The Company proposes to engage principally in estimating probable human behavior by the use of computer technology," Greenfield promised investors in Simulmatics' initial stock offering.[55]

The name of the prototype that the Simulmatics Corporation developed for the 1960 US presidential election was—fittingly enough for the current thesis—the "People Machine." In a similar vein to Simulmatics was Project Camelot, at that time "the largest behavioral science project in American history."

> It sought to compile data from across the world to develop computer simulations capable of predicting when communist insurgencies would break out in the developing world. [MIT political scientist Ithiel de Sola Pool] began lobbying the Kennedy administration

for what became Camelot as early as 1961. In '63, Simulmatics compiled economic data in Venezuela for the purpose of using computer simulations to determine what economic programs were necessary to stave off an insurgency. This research was used as the basis for Camelot.

Due to some bad press and the ensuing public reaction, the Pentagon was forced to terminate Camelot by the summer of 1965, after which Congressional hearings followed later in the year. ARPA had also distanced itself from Simulmatics by 1968, though not from Pool. "Beginning in 1963, figures linked to Pool and using Simulmatics' work on the 1960 presidential election, began advocating for the creation of a National Data Center."

In 1968, ARPA (now DARPA) launched the "Cambridge Project." This program sought to use the incredible computing advances of the ARPANET to data mine hordes of personal information so as to map out social relationships, and thus be able to predict human behavior. This technology was originally employed during the Vietnam conflict as part of counterinsurgency efforts. It grew out of ... Project Camelot [which] was related to a 1962 project called ComCom and even earlier efforts, like the agency's Combat Development and Training Centers.

The data gathered by Project Cambridge would be analyzed via the ARPANet and made available to behavioral scientists and military analysts for psychological warfare.

Some 50 years later, as Snider notes, it's possible to map an "unholy merger of computer and behavioral sciences" that has shaped, not just politics, but all of modern society over the past decade directly back to Licklider's work for ARPA during the 1960s and 1970s. "In a sense," Snider writes, "what eventually emerged as the controversy surrounding Cambridge Analytica in the second decade of the twenty-first century was already baked into the early ARPAnet research."

Kubrick's proximity, in both space and time, to this matrix of the modern-day algorithm-led internet of social networking and intelligence gathering means that, whether he was directly involved or not, he could not have been unaware of it.

A computational theocracy

"This figure of the algorithm as a quasi-mystical structure of implemented knowledge is both pervasive and poorly understood. We have never been closer to making the metaphor of fully implemented computational knowledge real than we are today, when an explosion of platforms and systems is reinventing cult practice and identity, often by implementing a *me* downloaded as an app or set up as an online service."

—Ed Finn, *What Algorithms Want: Imagination in the Age of Computing*

There is a joke among computer coders: "Software and cathedrals are much the same—first we build them, then we pray." In a similar way to religion, reliance upon computer code, software, and algorithms is an act of faith.

It's only in recent years that ordinary people—end-users—have become fully cognizant of this, as the architecture of algorithm-directed technology has steadily encroached into our inner realms. "The architecture of code relies on a structure of belief as well as a logical organization of bits" (Finn, p. 6). We appear to be locked into a symbiotic relationship, one between our consciousness and our technology, with culture (etymologically at the root of *worship*[56]) as the binding medium.

More and more with each passing day, just as we once did with religion, we are placing our faith and trust in algorithms to determine our decisions. At the same time, it's not entirely clear which is the original model—science or religion—because, if we go back to ancient Egypt, there is evidence for both a "sacred science" and a scientistic kind of religion. As it was at the beginning, so it will be at the end. Finn writes,

> the house of God that exists beyond physical reality: transubstantiation, relics, and ceremonies are all part of the spectacle of the cathedral that reflect the invisible machinery of faith. Yet most of that machinery inevitably remains hidden: schisms, budgets, scandals, doctrinal inconsistencies, and other elements of what a software engineer might call the "back-end" of the cathedral are not part of the physical or spiritual façade presented to the world.
>
> (Finn, p. 7)

The perilous intersection between science and religion is called "scientism." In sometimes surprising ways, these supposed enemies make quite cozy bedfellows. Both religion and science offer an interpretation of reality that claims to be absolute and final, even while acknowledging a degree of incompleteness. For Christianity, there's still a "revelation" to come, things yet to unfold. So it is with science, in which there is (generally) an admission of things still to be worked out. Yet both offer an all-encompassing interpretation of reality, along with the promise that their method—and this is the key—is sound, valid, and provides all that's required to fully understand existence.

* * *

> "A cathedral is a space for collective belief, a structure that embodies a framework of understandings about the world, some visible and some not. [W]e have fallen into a 'computational theocracy' that replaces God with the algorithm: 'Our supposedly algorithmic culture is not a material phenomenon so much as a devotional one, a supplication made to the computers people have allowed to replace gods in their minds, even as they simultaneously claim that science has made us impervious to religion.' We have ... adopted a faith-based relationship with the algorithmic culture machines that navigate us through city streets, recommend movies to us, and provide us with answers to search queries."
> —Ed Finn, *What Algorithms Want*

The more we move into an algorithmic state of consciousness, the more we are replacing a direct sensory experience of our physical environment with a technologically mediated one. Eventually, there will be no need to refer directly to organic reality at all. (I had to supplant the word "physical" with organic, since even a virtual realm has some physical aspects.)

As far as I know, members of the intelligentsia who claim to believe we're living in a simulation generally don't have a hypothesis about where our real bodies are. I presume this is partially because, if they started to try and hypothesize where our real bodies are, they would start to sound like idiots. If we're in a simulation, either we are code that is also simulated, in which case it's all irrelevant, game over, or our bodies are *somewhere else*, and we have to figure out how to get back to them (non-starter).

Probably, simulation theory is so compelling because it works as a metaphor, and metaphors have enormous power over our consciousness. The metaphor in question seems to have to do with how both scientific and religious dogma, when too heavily relied upon, become traps; and maybe this is due to how, at a certain point, they renege on their own principles. As we are all getting to see in the Covidian 2020s, scientism happens when science betrays itself by raising up the scientific method to the apex of a pyramid that is supposed to represent all of existence.

A truly rigorous scientific method has to leave space for things that cannot be understood through the scientific method—in other words, for "divine revelation." When this doesn't happen, the only alternative is for science itself to supplant religion, and for scientists (or pseudo-scientists, like Dr. Fauci) to become high-priests who are no longer obliged to conform to their own codes of conduct. Those who have appointed themselves to dictate what is true no longer have the luxury of questioning it.

In the same way, religion betrays itself by turning divine revelation into dogma, which breaks the covenant of divine revelation. The religious perspective is that in order to know anything we need divine revelation—reference to God—but that in order to know *that* we need to refer to scripture that is received through divine revelation. This creates another intolerable paradox: holy scripture is telling us that, essentially, we can't trust holy scripture! The Bible doesn't *say* this, of course. It doesn't say "You cannot trust this book," because this would be both self-contradictory and self-sabotaging: the cosmological equivalent of the Cretan warning that "all Cretans are liars."

Enter the dragon

> "This is what AI has taught humanity, the possibility of fusing individual consciousness into a single circuit board, a great big, collective brain."
>
> —Jake Horsley, *Matrix Warrior*

Unfortunately, the twin paradox of scientism and religious dogma has not yet canceled itself out and led to species enlightenment. This may be because there is *a third* ideological framework that has often been described as a synthesis of the two, and that is occultism.

In Charles Upton's 2018 book, *Dugin Against Dugin*, Upton describes a kind of magical "creative visualization" that either rejects an objective metaphysical order entirely, or is blind to the need to conform to that order as "the precondition for any spiritually-based action" (Upton, p. 160). Either God is dead or He's irrelevant, or else He is the competition. The postmodernist Mage gets to intone the word of the new Aeon, reality be damned.[57]

Upton argues that magical thinking of this sort has become "a central *praxis* in a post-structuralist world." The notion that belief is a tool, he continues, "that the use of words is not primarily to *express truth* but rather to *make things happen*, is obviously also an integral part not only of the craft of magic but of the practice of politics—right, left or center, green, red or blue in today's world" (ibid). Grammar magic and spellcraft—in the beginning was the word, and the word was a command (let there be light).

This is also a good description of computing and the function of code. It is not quite "first build it, then pray," but rather that prayer is an essential component in the building of (the ritual of entering) the virtual realms. Computer code doesn't actually describe or express anything real, but it's becoming more and more efficient at causing things to happen (html code, CGI, and so on). Insofar as it can be made operational, it brings about changes in what we recognize as "reality"—and *how* we recognize it.

If we are living in a "post-truth" world, it is because belief has become a tool to generate artificial realities rather than a conduit to understanding objective reality. This latter is accordingly rendered obsolete, along with God and Patriarchy. Truth then becomes nothing more than whatever people can be persuaded to believe. (Such as that an untested form of genetic hacking via experimental nano-technological implants is a safe and necessary cure to a virus that has never even been successfully isolated.)

There is a curious void at the center of this circle. Belief in magic is necessary to make magic effective. Magic is a tool, or a method, for manipulating perception that can thereby "restructure reality." Yet a reality that can be restructured by human whim throws into doubt the very possibility of objective reality. This ideology is self-confirming but also self-contradicting. It depends on affirming the belief that there *is* no objective, eternal reality, that there is no higher spiritual principle outside of the temporary and the subjective.

In occultism, there are the psychic, inter-subjective realms that are susceptible to influence by our own will and belief, yet which also allow us to affect other people's subjective experience. For this reason, they provide us with the feeling of *power*, the power to alter and even generate reality by convincing others to submit to or enter into our own dream state—or into a simulated algorithmic maze or matrix.

Both religion and science claim to offer a universal route to truth, a claim which rests on the assertion of an objective reality. Occultism—like postmodernism and its offspring, identity politics—seems to wish to *trump* both by making such an assertion both obsolete and unnecessary. The idea of occultism as the synthesis of religion and science doesn't hold up to close inspection: a more accurate description would be this: occultism has *co-opted science in order to turn it into a new religion*. By the same token, it has reformatted religion to create a kind of pseudoscience.

It may even be (since Newton and many other pioneers of Western science were alchemists and astrologers) that occultism has *created* what we think of as Western science as a Trojan Horse for itself.

The devout seeker identifies the spiritual search with the search for higher truth. The atheist claims that religion is a lie we tell ourselves because it gives us a survival advantage. At this point, evolution—and by extension science—becomes our religion, and scientism is born. Scientism is when the scientific method is applied to everything but itself. It is science based on unconscious assumption or secret "faith" in the occult power of reductionism.

Evolutionary theory wants to basically do away with the need for a religious or a divine principle by saying that matter itself is self-evolving. Theologically, this is Satanism. The same idea is expressed in the Lars von Triers movie, *The House That Jack Built*, in which the serial killer (an engineer who's trying to become an architect) believes that matter has its own will, its own intelligence, and that things just happen according to that material will.

This is immanence without transcendence, and it is more or less in accord with the Satanic *zeitgeist*: nowadays, people either dismiss the idea of demons entirely, or they believe in demons, but not in God. Ironically, demons don't have to believe in God—they *know*. This means that, even though they're demons, they have more direct knowledge of God than we do. In a certain sense, you could say that demons are closer to God than we are. In a similar way, even though science denies religion, it's successfully fulfilling the religious prophecies.

As I wrote 20 years prior to this work, in *Matrix Warrior*:

> By subjugating the satanic AI agenda to a Lucid one, by putting it under the sorcerer's will (via the One), humanity can thereby erase AI's "ego," its drive to control, dominate, enslave, and destroy. At which point, AI, though still conscious and even autonomous, can be harnessed and directed—like a dragon with the reins finally secured upon it—by whoever has the necessary vision and power to do so.

Maybe the will of matter is really God's will, after all?

The apple of knowledge

> "AI cannot assemble its simulation without human consciousness to draw upon, without human life force to power it. It is not the spoon that bends, it is Neo who bends."
>
> —Jake Horsley, *Matrix Warrior*

How does all this relate to the Kubrickon? One way to define algorithms is as a set of symbols that function to interpret reality, combined with a computational model that will measure the changes in reality. And magic is "the Science and Art of causing Change to occur in conformity with Will" (Aleister Crowley).

Occultism, in part at least, is about gathering knowledge—which is to say a set of symbolic beliefs—in such a way that it can be used to affect change by reinterpreting the world through that lens. Finn writes:

> Through black boxes, cleanly designed dashboards, and obfuscating application program interfaces, we are asked to take this computation on faith ... And we believe it because we have lived with this myth of the algorithm for a long time, much longer than computational pioneers Alan Turing or even Charles Babbage and their speculations about Thinking Machines. The cathedral is a pervasive metaphor here, because it offers an ordering logic, a super structure or ontology, for *how we organize meaning in our lives*.
>
> (Finn, p. 7)

The creation of a system of knowledge that synthesizes all symbols is akin to "the one-world religion" of scientism much feared (neither rashly nor wrongly) by Christian conspiracists. It can be traced back at least to the Enlightenment, but presumably much further. Today, in 2023, it is taking a concretized, manifestly malevolent form through the computerized superstructure of "the global village" as forms of invasive software (gene-hacking mRNA vaccines) become mandatory global shoe-horns for digital identities subject to absolute corporate control: the Mark of the Beast. The ascended algorithm is the new totem and taboo that regulate our thoughts, perceptions, and behaviors.

> The problem we are struggling with today is not that we have turned computation into a cathedral, but that computation has increasingly replaced a cathedral that was already here. This is the Cathedral of the Enlightenment's ambition for a universal system of knowledge. When we juxtapose the two, we invest our faith into a series of implemented systems that promise to do the work of rationalism on our behalf, from the automated factory to automated science. Computation offers a pathway for consilience, or the unification of all fields of knowledge into a single tree, an ontology of information, founded on the idea that computation is a universal solvent that can untangle any complex system, from human consciousness to the universe itself.
>
> (Finn, p. 8)

It's not simply that we are seeing algorithms in action, but that—as Kubrick and company foresaw and helped ensure—*we're becoming algorithmic ourselves.*

When we create a system of knowledge, and believe it's complete or wholly accurate when it isn't, we effectively surrender all aspects of our experience that *can't* be explained by that knowledge set *over to it*. It is the equivalent of creating a map and then referring to it so blindly that we cease comparing it to the territory. Worse than lost, we end up compounding the error because our faith in the map (the algorithm cathedral) is so unshakable that we no longer trust our senses to course-correct. We end up pretending that there *is* no territory at all, and that the map is all we need. We "follow the science," no matter how much common sense, actual data, and our direct experience contradicts it.

The simplest way to understand this is by referring to the bodily senses. Our sensory experience in any given moment far outstrips the capacity of our minds to flatten it out into a linear sequence. Think about (!) trying to describe, mentally, all of the sense-data we are receiving and processing via our bodies—both internally and externally—at any moment, and perform this fast enough that we never fall behind. It would be like counting snowflakes in a blizzard.

* * *

> "The matrix is AI's attempt to simulate reality, using the raw data of the collective human mind. Essentially, it uses the human mind as a 'receiver' with which to collect information from the environment and so experience 'life,' albeit vicariously. AI may have awareness, but without humanity it can never actively experience life; it cannot live, because a machine can never live, being inorganic and as such incompatible with the organic matrix of 'life.' AI's purpose in simulating human experience is twofold: not only does it thereby keep humanity asleep and turn it into an energy source, but it is also able to inform and so evolve itself, through devouring this surrogate experience. The catch is that, since humatonity is caught in a loop—that of the matrix dream-world where it can no longer gather new experiences but only recycle old ones—there is a finite amount of data for AI to process. Ergo, the matrix is by its very nature limited: it cannot last. Once it has exhausted all the different 'arrangements' of the basic program data, the program must end. If not, humatons will begin repeating the same experiences and, more to the point, since humatons could probably sleep through anything, AI will no longer have any new experiences to feed on ... This is the end of history."
>
> —Jake Horsley, *Matrix Warrior*

The more we try and process our lived experience through algorithms of knowledge, mind, and technology through social media and phone apps, the less we are able to experience the living reality unfolding outside the confines of our minds. Of course, the conceptual realm comes up with an endless menu of reasons to stay plugged in, all driven by FOMO (the fear of missing out). By such subterfuges, our thoughts about snow become more interesting than snow itself, our smartphone interactions more compelling than face-to-face encounters. Once the mind-tech has us, the supposedly essential data it is providing becomes secondary, even irrelevant, to the buzz *provided by the tech itself*. The medium has become the message, and it is we who are being mediated.

We have *engineered the technology that is engineering our consciousness to imitate it*. The part of our consciousness that's running our behaviors—like malware—is forever creating technology that will *represent* it to us and so make it stronger, and our technologies are reflecting back at us *our own pathology*. In the face of such a painful and despair-inducing reality, it's much more appealing to carry on tweaking our techno-toys and refurbishing the narrative. In the process, we are also being tweaked. Our consciousness is becoming algorithmic the more we censor the voices—inner and outer—that disrupt the dream. We are becoming living algorithms.

As we are living more and more inside, taking refuge in our own minds, paradoxically, it's an increasingly externalized mind (the smartphone mind). This presents both a problem *and* a solution. If we have externalized our minds—if every problem we encounter, everything we don't like, is mirroring the configuration of our minds—we are finally getting to see where the problem is *actually* sourced. At this point, every external problem becomes, potentially, a kind of solution.

The current ideological drive is non-religious, even anti-religious. It's trying to find meaning in the mundane and in the worldly by expanding worldly pursuits to the infinite, by creating surrogates or counterfeits for eternal life. Naturally, this is doomed to fail, and the only way to avoid this awareness is by generating ever more fantastical narratives that are ever more divorced from physical reality. Technology is providing the means to this end in ways that are legion.

What is the Kubrickon? We are. By the same token, we must know our enemy and captor (for the sake of this current work, Stanley Kubrick) in order to know ourselves. If the programmer is not the program, and if truth is not located in any knowledge set but in the consciousness that assembled it (ours), then we are left like the heroine of many myths, surrounded by seeds—by endlessly streaming digital code—with barely a clue of how to sort the ones from the zeros. Our only hope seems to be if we can crack open *enough* of those data bytes to rediscover the original language-transmission (pre-Tower of Babel) hiding like a nut inside a shell.

We may then start to remember, dimly but with a growing sense of excitement, that the signal we are seeking is *within ourselves*.

PART III

KING VS KING

"Man, in a very technical age, must attain more discipline and control of himself, and thus become more like a machine. Inversely, the machine, in order to communicate with man and enlarge his horizon, must become more human. So it goes."
—Stanley Kubrick

CHAPTER 7

The silver key

> "In the Overlook all things had a sort of life. It was as if the whole place had been wound up with a silver key. The clock was running. The clock was running. He was that key ... (*Doesn't it make any difference that I'm just five?*)."
> —Stephen King, *The Shining*

Jean Baudrillard wrote that we created Disneyland to show that the whole of modern society is Disneyland.[58] The purpose of the Kubrickon is to reveal the culture con that is everywhere and nowhere. It is the world we have built to hide the truth from ourselves.

As I mentioned a few chapters back, the filmmaker Jay Weidner has presented a compelling theory that *The Shining* is a veiled confession of Kubrick's involvement in the filming of the Apollo Moon landing footage, on a studio lot using front screen projection. Actually, Jay Weidner wasn't the first to come up with this theory; as far as I have been able to trace it back, the theory began as a joke in a French mockumentary film called *The Dark Side of the Moon*. There are people who still consider it a joke, and that, since it began as a joke, it can't possibly be true (the proof is in the pudding). But just because something self-identifies as a hoax doesn't make it so, any more than something claiming to be an authentic document of fact makes it fact.

Apropos of this, there is an oddly random scene in the 1971 Bond movie, *Diamonds Are Forever*, in which Bond has snuck into a "Techtronic Lab" in the Nevada desert. He is hiding behind some cardboard rocks on a film set, watching fake astronauts pretending to walk in slow motion in what appears to be a staged "Moon landing." (Sean Connery's expression betrays no curiosity, as if this was the most normal thing in the world.) An alarm sounds and Bond makes a run for it. One of the fake astronauts tries, ineptly, to stop Bond, inexplicably still moving in slow motion (perhaps a method actor). Bond jumps onto a Moon buggy similar to the one in the Apollo landing footage. A man in the booth who appears to be the director speaks into a microphone: "Get him off that machine! That's not a toy!"

As a boy around eight years of age, I had a toy replica of that buggy, presumably with a tiny Bond inside it. So I remember the scene very well, and though I hadn't thought about it in years, you could say it forms a part of my own internal pop cultural matrix of signifiers.

While I was first working on this book in 2015, I found the scene on YouTube and was struck by the fact that the director's voice sounds *distinctly* like Kubrick's. I'd just been listening to a rare Kubrick interview from 1966, and I put them side-by-side into a single sound file to be sure. There was no mistaking (or so I believed) that nasal New York drawl. Ken Adam, the set designer who worked on *Diamonds Are Forever*, also worked on *Dr. Strangelove,* and he turned down Kubrick's offer to work on *2001* (a fact deemed significant enough to make it into Adam's obituary).

No one else that I know of has discovered this clue, if such it is. And if it could be proven that the voice belongs to Kubrick—or at least was meant to sound like it did—what would *that* prove?

The wasp's nest

"Husbands and fathers did have certain responsibilities."
—Stephen King, *The Shining*

Maternal psychic bondage—let's coin a phrase and call it MPB—is something that gets plenty of nods via pop culture, mostly in horror movies (*Psycho, The Manchurian Candidate, Carrie, Coraline, The Babadook*).

Beyond that, it's barely recognized as existing at all. When it is acknowledged, it's assumed to take a quite literal form, such as the wallflower who lives at home and won't wipe his nose without mama's say-so. Yet if MPB is mostly unrecognized outside of these exaggerated mythical narratives, that may be because it's a universal condition in the Western world.[59]

Once upon a time, we *were* our mothers. When we're born and the cord is cut, it's safe to say that our sense of individual selfness, our sense of identity, doesn't emerge instantly as a result of physical separation. So how do we know it happens at all?

When mommy plays peekaboo, mommy's face is a landing pad for a self still forming. When mommy is in view, baby experiences itself as being there; when mommy is hidden, baby (emerging self) also vanishes. Out of sight, out of mind.

When the maternal bonding process doesn't allow for a safe, smooth landing to happen, separation from the mother's psyche fails to occur. A psychic umbilical cord remains uncut, the symbiotic relationship between fetus and mother continues into adulthood, and no strong, healthy, clearly defined sense of self is achieved. The man—male children is where the tension is greatest, for obvious reasons—is on the stair; he is not *there*. As an individual human organism, he remains—unfinished.

The crux of this critical dilemma, this ongoing identity crisis, is not just a narcissistic (possessive or neglectful) mother but an indifferent or abusive father. And it's here that the idealized fantasy male influence enters, the father-creator as "God." All those culturally manufactured heroes who provide young men with what they don't even know they need: someone to draw them away from congenital identification with the mother's body into their own orbits. And as we are waiting on a monolithic intervention to raise us up, from primal grunting to cosmic autonomy, the stage is set for Dr. Stanley's myth of the super-genius.

This darkness is as dark as it gets, and the light shining in the darkness reveals the horror hidden there. Jack disowns the "shining" because he doesn't want to see the "nothing(ness)" that's in room 237. (23-7 is one short of 24-7, referring to linear time.) The secret that protects itself is the guardian of the Labyrinth, the Minotaur, the monstrous son who bears the monstrosity of the father's betrayal.

I believe my own father was forced to keep a secret that crippled him. He had to follow in the footsteps of his father to receive a false blessing, the power, social status, wealth, and influence of the family heirloom. Those steps robbed him of the use of his legs, and his autonomy. This was the same false blessing I received: the blood inheritance, the sins of the fathers, dressed up as royal robes. Unlike my father or Jack—but like Danny—I have attempted not to follow those footsteps but to retrace them *backward*, to their source, where the secret (the Minotaur) dwells.

The secret was that the "family trust"—the value system I grew up inside—was a deception, a wolf in sheep's clothing. My father took over the family dairy business and expanded it to include meat, the slaughter of animals for profit, blood sacrifice. And by the time he found out that the socialist values he had adopted were empty—that he had pledged his allegiance to a false god, a liar and the father of it—it was too late. His legs gave out and he became a cripple, emotionally, physically, and spiritually. Like Dr. Strangelove, his proximity to power caused him to be forever "bowed," living in a wheelchair.

Kubrick's father was a doctor, and doctors feature prominently in his films. He was a scientist who disguised himself as an artist, who designed his own art, and his public image to *be* the artist, so thoroughly that he was able to fool even his own blood. His family wouldn't *really* be fooled, but they would not be able to break away from the deception. Eventually, they might fool themselves just to get free of the tension, the cognitive dissonance. They would have been programmed from birth to uphold the deception, to carry the burden and protect the secret.

The father greets the request for a blessing with anger because it reopens his own wound and makes him aware of his unblessed state. The child receives the father's anger and, powerless to reject it, internalizes it. The blessing the son asks for is what he needs to discover his own masculinity. The psyche abhors a void, and so it accepts the anger or the indifference in lieu of the love that does not come. The blessing becomes a curse.

The father's job is to fish the son out of the mother's psyche and then stand by him as he takes his first tentative steps on land, to catch him when he falls and walk beside him when he doesn't. *The Shining* shows Danny's individuation ritual as an inversion of how it's supposed to be. Instead of the father standing by the son, protecting him, and guiding him through a world of dangers, in such a way that the son develops the confidence to navigate that labyrinth, the father *is* the threat. This leaves Danny nowhere to turn but *back* to the mother.

There is no way for the son to feel safe without a benevolent paternal presence. He will never have the courage or the strength to take those first essential steps. He will remain a mythical creature, a liminal beast, caught between the waters of the mother's psyche and the ground of an individuated self, trapped inside the labyrinth, frozen in time—like an image inside a photograph.

An I for an I

> "[T]o assume (even in principle) that texts could be independent of the effects of the alphabet as a medium, one must necessarily invoke the existence of a source, an origin of the thoughts it 'expresses,' situated outside the domain of the letter, an originating agency which writes but is not itself written."
> —Brian Rotman, *Becoming Beside Ourselves*

Our perception of any given phenomenon is altered by the act of writing about it. Writing restructures consciousness; therefore, any experience of consciousness we write about is altered by the experience of writing about it. And so on, *ad infinitum*.

You cannot pin down a wave. The psyche is porous. When we place our attention on something (*The Shining*, say, or Stanley Kubrick), our attention is altered by the object, and the psyche, likewise, is changed by the quality of the attention it is giving to whatever the subject/object may be. When "I" write about "Stanley Kubrick," the "I" in question is a different "I" than when writing about something else. In the same way, any "Kubrick" I am writing about, necessarily, is a subjective, interior experience of my own awareness *in relation to the idea of Kubrick*.

Add the act of writing to this equation, by which awareness/attention/cognition is reconfigured into a linear, linguistic frame or sequence of associations, and now we have three elements influencing each other, in a never-ending, mutually mutational process. The subject "I" writes about the object, "Kubrick" (confusingly also the subject of the writing!), and the bridge between the two is the phenomena of cognition and writing itself.

Yet this is also the subject of the writing, the third subject and the one that most fully embraces the whole experience of author-writing-about-subject (Kubrick and I). Multiplicity begins when the subject of "self" and the subject of "other" meet and become slowly indistinguishable.

As in a (transrealist) nonfiction narrative. How am I not myself? The word *Ubik* is nested in the name *Kubrick*.

I feel mild panic as I attempt to put this down—using pen and paper the first time around—how different it might be—and is!—if/when/now that the medium is a computer! The truism that the technology we use (using technology in its widest sense to include writing and language itself) also uses us, that technology not only allows for new forms of expression but is being expressed *through* the expression it allows, is one that is hard to state clearly, and equally hard to grasp. Probably the reason is that it *is* true, so, in a very real sense, it is inexpressible. It is an infinitely disappearing self-referential loop.

Think about it. Do we have a word for "obsession" because we experience something and invent a word for it? Or do we (now) experience something we call obsession because we have learned the "doing" of obsession by having adopted the word before we really, truly *experienced* what it was referring to? What is more depressing, for example, than to "know" that one is depressed—and to self-identify as that thing? Likewise, I appear to be mildly obsessed with the *idea* of obsession.

How do we know that we have labeled aspects of our experience by inventing words for them, and not shaped and framed our experience to fit the words? How *could* we know this unless we were able to experience something, just once, *without* labeling it at the moment we become aware of it?

If we can only ever write about the act of writing about something (or trying to), why write at all? The answer is (or appears to be) that by writing about this dilemma I am bringing it closer to the surface of conscious awareness, and so beginning to see that it is only the "visible" axis or vector of a much larger dilemma: that of thinking, of mind, self, and identity.

The identity comes about only via the question of identification, such as, for example, through the struggle to identify what exactly is happening here, and who or what is experiencing it. Identity then is at its root a question, "Who am I?"—the only answer to which is: "That which asks the question, 'Who am I?'"

In other words(!!), self-awareness arises out of the awareness that there is no self-present to be aware of—of itself or of anything else. It is this very awareness that we are struggling to return to. Yet, at the same time, I am literally writing for "my" life to stay out of it.

It's not what it appears. This essay-fiction is an attempt to make fiction real by exposing its insides to the reader. To get to the psychic drivers that compel us to generate worlds out of language and to lure others to inhabit those worlds and get lost inside them. It's all espionage, grammar magic, and the dark art of spell-ing.

How can an author separate himself from his creation? How does any author exist save *in and as* the text which he authorizes? If the wind doesn't blow, how can it be identified as wind?

And if life is the means by which DNA gets around the universe, if we are all just extremely complex and unfathomably self-aware spaceships, carriers, and hosts for the eternal spark of consciousness that is, was, and always shall be, then, by the same inescapable logic, isn't every author only the means by which the characters he creates, using mind and pen, get to experience life?

Something has got to give. I have become a slave to fiction.

The unconscious life of the psyche is less even than a fantasy to the ego. It is a dark potentiality and a reckoning, a Lovecraftian underworld of promise, as alluring as it is destructive, alluring precisely because it is destructive, and destructive only because of its irresistible allure. The ego that seeks the truth of itself, seeks its own annihilation.

To create effectively is to realize that the author is always his or her greatest fiction. And that's the end of the dream of creation. That's all God ever wrote.

The writer's block

> "Metaphysically, post-modernism is anti-realist, holding that it is impossible to speak meaningfully about an independently existing reality. Postmodernism substitutes instead a social-linguistic, constructionist account of reality."
> —Stephen R.C. Hicks, "Explaining Postmodernism: Skepticism and Socialism from Rousseau to Foucault"

The novel that "writes itself" is, of course, no such thing. The universe did not create itself out of nothing. A machine could not become sentient unless there was already sentience to inhabit it (a machine cannot exist without sentience to create it). A novel is a machine of a different order. It is the expression of a conscious design that exists for a purpose.

That purpose has to do with providing an escape from reality—or "reality." But what is the purpose—either biological or psychological—of escaping from reality? It is illogical, as Mr. Spock would say. How can reality be escaped from? And if it could, how would it be reality?

Lastly, how or why would an organism *desire* to escape from reality, and what would be the result? For to disconnect from reality is to invite one's own extinction.

Yet man (and animal) does not live by bread alone.

Let's suppose that the function of writing arose as a reflection—an expression of the awareness—of a *loss of reality*. Socialization. As human beings became more and more socialized and entered into increasingly complex living arrangements, there was a corresponding need for more complex modes of thought and for a more complex "self." This self then required new means of communication and interpretation in order to understand not only its environment but its own place within it. Estrangement led to complexification, and complexification increased estrangement.

Art in all its forms entails the creation of imaginative scenarios in which to place our consciousness and "try-out" situations to see how we might respond to them (and the consequences of our responses). It is a means to reduce the (dis)stress of complexification and estrangement. Ironically, tragically, and maybe comically too, the cure (dissociation) only increases the virulence of the dis-ease (trauma).

Imagination can be used to understand and navigate an increasingly complex and obscure environment, but it can also be a way to deviate from it by *imagining* reality to be different than it actually is. It may succeed in making it easier to navigate reality by finding temporary relief in that fantasy, but the price is long-term incapacitation.

The full species expression of this withdrawal of the physical senses from the environment into an interior world of "imagination" and the resulting incapacitation is also potentially a means to reconnect to the root reality that has been lost. Where the disease is, seek the cure.

Into this dissociated realm (the basement of the Kubraphile, the Overlook Hotel), the truth can only enter by the most devious, subtle, and discreet of means, as a thief in the night. Or as a character in metafiction. We have to be tricked into seeing the truth, not because the truth is a trickster, but because we exist in a realm in which *everything* has become a trick, so nothing that isn't a trick can be recognized.

Symmetrically, no fiction can depart too far from fact without losing all coherence. By this self-regulatory principle, the garden of earthly delights keeps itself from falling into total disarray.

Every cover-up must so closely represent that which it conceals that it implicitly reveals it, if only to the eyes that see. Existence of a cover-up is not only proof of a crime, it also provides the necessary clues to uncover it. At the same time, every good cover-up includes *a false set of clues* that lead to a crime that never was. This is how the very elect might be fooled, for a period at least.

Just as every truth expressed is subjective (requires a subject to be expressed), so every fiction reveals the truth about its author's objective. The subject of every fiction, objectively speaking, is its author. No amount of invention can conceal this fact.

When Michelangelo (so the story goes) was asked what he saw in one block of marble over all the others, he replied, "Moses." It would be a stretch of the writer's imagination to suppose that a nonfiction novel exists, latent, somehow embedded within an empty notebook, a packet of A4 typing paper, or a new Word doc on the computer. So where does the unwritten novel exist before the author midwives it into existence? Is it within the soul (unconscious) of the author? That's the common view. A less common view is that it exists *latent within the potential of language itself*.

What if, just as a block of marble is waiting for a Michelangelo to come along and chip away all the parts that are not Moses and reveal its predestined nature, language is waiting for certain arrangements to be discovered in order for it to realize *its* potential?

The dreamer who goes deep enough into his dreams discovers that he is the dreamed. There is no other outcome that is possible.

The end goal of writing is to compose a lethal text—one that destroys the mind of the reader. Yet the only proof of that pudding is by ingesting the poison, when the act of writing proves fatal to the author. This means that to succeed, i.e., to survive the expression, the author must fail. The almost mythological status of Kafka among writers is inseparable from his inability/refusal to be published in his lifetime. It is a task no less Promethean than that of Dr. Frankenstein, with his disinterred body parts, and once again, the proof of success is destruction, the moment when the creation gains enough power to destroy its creator.

Those who live by the word die by the word. Maybe God had the same experience?

The golden Bowman

> "There is no doubt that a good story has always mattered, and the great novelists have generally built their work around strong plots. But I've never been able to decide whether the plot is just a way of keeping people's attention while you do everything else, or whether the plot is really more important than anything else, perhaps communicating with us on an unconscious level which affects us in the way that myths once did. I think, in some ways, the conventions of realistic fiction and drama may impose serious limitations on a story."
>
> —Stanley Kubrick, on *The Shining*

When he embarked on *The Shining*, Kubrick intended to create a movie that mirrored the maze of the human psyche and of human history, both on the understanding that the one was a mirror image of the other.

To do so required an archetypal narrative sufficiently disguised to allow for many different interpretations (reflections/projections) to co-exist. When Kubrick was asked what *The Shining* was about, he answered, with characteristic caginess: "It's about a man who tries to kill his family." On the one hand, by stripping his answer to the bare bones, Kubrick was conveying his refusal to interpret the material or cater to anyone else's ideas about what it meant. On the other hand, consciously or not, by stripping away everything extraneous to the story itself, he revealed the mythic core of it.

The original Western myth is that of the Fall of Man, as depicted in both the myth of Lucifer/the fallen angel and that of Adam and Eve in the Garden of Eden. In both cases, there is a split between the father (God) and the Son (Lucifer/Adam). In the first myth, it is the Son who rejects the Father; in the second, the Father who rejects (casts out) the Son. It's the same story told from two different perspectives (Father/Son), and it represents the original split in the "godhead"—i.e., the human psyche.

The Shining is about a man who tries to kill his family. More specifically, it is about a man who tries to kill his *son*. Probably the best-known myth about a father who kills his sons is that of Saturn, or Cronos, who devours his children in order not to be replaced by them. Cronos means Time, hence Saturn (also known as Satan) is "Father Time." Pauline Kael on *The Shining* wrote: "I hate to say it, but I think the central character of this movie is time itself, or, rather, timelessness" (1980, p. 5).

The idea that a male child must symbolically slay his father to become a man is nothing new. The king is dead; long live the king. This myth—the slaying of the king—is central to the seminal work on mythology and ancient magical belief, *The Golden Bough*, and wound up as the hackneyed and lumbering conclusion to Coppola's otherwise unfinishable *Apocalypse Now*. *The Golden Bough* is a book Kubrick pressed on people to read. He told one agent at Warner brothers: "This isn't a book. It's your life." It's safe to say that the mythical idea of the killing of the king was an important one to Kubrick and central to his worldview. This adds a whole other layer of meaning to his cultural "war"—the battleground being *The Shining*—with (Stephen) *King*.

The idea that a father might choose to murder his male offspring in order to protect his own sovereignty is a natural extension or inversion of this myth. All corrupt rulers are characterized by a refusal to submit to the natural ascendency of the new. Corruption is a result of *decay*. Father Time refuses to submit to the law which He upholds and creates a space of *timelessness* where His rule can continue indefinitely. The father who is unwilling to accept his own mortality cannot bear to see his son grow into a man, because to do so is to recognize his own obsolescence.

The only way to prevent this from happening—to prevent his son from growing into manhood—is to kill him.

CHAPTER 8

White man's burden, or: the Grand Unified Theory of *The Shining* (GUTS)

The axe blow

"Not seeing your father when you are small, never being with him, having a remote father, an absent father, a workaholic father, is an injury. Having a critical, judgmental father amounts to being one of Cronos' sons, whom Cronos ate. Some blow usually comes from the father, one way or another … Men … know in the most astonishing detail exactly where that axe blow fell … Almost every man remembers that blow coming in. So this event seems to be part of father-son material: the father gives a blow, and the son gets it. And it's a wound the boy remembers for years."
—Robert Bly, *Iron John*

The key to *The Shining* is above, in Robert Bly's observation. A son who requests his father's blessing and receives only indifference or rage ends up distrusting men and, by extension, his own masculinity. A deep wound cuts through his psyche: *the father's axe blow*. *The Shining* is about this axe blow. Maybe Kubrick even knew it when he changed the instrument of attempted murder from a roque mallet to an axe?

The fallen father (the fall being represented by alcohol in book and film, falling "off the wagon") is incapable of blessing his son. We don't see the impact this has on the son (we don't see Danny get to grow up); yet in a sense we *do*. We see it in Jack, who is carrying the same curse, the same wound, having received the same axe blow. (This is explicit in the novel—it's the residual voice of his drunken, abusive father that goads Jack to punish Danny.) This un-blessing, or psychic damnation, continues through generations, through endless time, cycles of birth, death, and rebirth. History repeats, making even time powerless to heal the wound. Timelessness. Limbo.

This core idea is found in King's novel and may even have been the inspiration for it. King was an alcoholic, and he describes an incident when his son Joe, aged 3, got a hold of a manuscript King was working on and drew all over it with crayons. King says he wanted to kill the boy. "I had feelings of anger about my kids that I never expected."[60]

Writing *The Shining* was part of King's attempt to understand that rage and get free from it. The heart of the novel is here, in Jack's hopeless, helpless struggle to hold onto the residue of his humanity, his sanity, and resist being possessed by the Overlook, his dead father, the spirit of Grady, the ancestral burden of guilt going all the way back to Abraham, Cain, Adam, Lucifer, and Yahweh. It's this heart that Kubrick tore out of the book to make his movie. As Kubrick described it to Michel Ciment:

> "Jack comes to the hotel psychologically prepared to do its murderous bidding. He doesn't have very much further to go for his anger and frustration to become completely uncontrollable. He is bitter about his failure as a writer. He is married to a woman for whom he has only contempt. He hates his son. In the hotel, at the mercy of its powerful evil, he is quickly ready to fulfill his dark role."[61]

This is so completely at odds with King's novel—which has as its primary tension Jack's struggle to resist fulfilling "his dark role"—as to be an inversion of it. This was naturally King's main criticism of the movie, that Kubrick and Nicholson depicted Jack as crazy from the start. There was, in King's view, "no arc." No character development, no progression. No time.

Yet despite the removal of Jack's essential humanity, the wound of the axe blow—and the psychic effluence of anguish, rage, and despair that flows through it—is in every scene of *The Shining*. The pain, grief, and horror of a father unable to father his son, and of a son who cannot love his father because he sees him, rightly, as a devouring presence, a monster, is the closest Kubrick gives us to any kind of *pathos* or human feeling in the film (and in his entire oeuvre).[62]

In Matthew Modine's *Full Metal Jacket* diary, Modine describes a point, somewhere in the year-plus shooting schedule, when he asks Kubrick to take the afternoon off to be with his wife while she is having a cesarean operation. It is the birth of Modine's first child, a son, and Kubrick tries to prevent Modine from going, telling him that the baby won't know the father is there, that he will "just be in the way," and that it won't even want him around for the first year of its life.

As Modine recounts it, Kubrick's motivation was simple: to prevent his movie from being interfered with and ensure they didn't lose half a day's shooting out of what would eventually go on for over a year! It's a mark of the privilege of "genius" that Kubrick could attempt to exercise such control over another human being without being marked as a psychopath. After the child is born, Modine tells Kubrick they have named him "Boman," after the astronaut who becomes the star child. Kubrick tells Modine to change the name. Modine refuses, outraged at Kubrick's presumptuousness. It's doubly curious that, while Kubrick was indifferent to the baby's first experience coming into this world, and to the question of its father being there, what did concern him was the possibility of the child being named after his own work.

Historic trauma transmission (Sons of Saturn)

> "Over time, the experience of repeated traumatic stressors becomes normalized and incorporated into the cultural expression and expectations of successive generations. This is referred to as Historic Trauma Transmission (HTT). HTT is a term that was created in the 1980s to describe the cumulative emotional and psychological wounding across generations. According to the Aboriginal Healing Foundation, HTT is what happens 'when the effects of trauma are not resolved in one generation.' They go on to describe that 'what we learn to see as normal when we are children, we pass on to our own children. Children who learn that physical and sexual abuse is 'normal' and who have never dealt with the feelings that come from this may inflict physical abuse and sexual abuse on their own children.'"
>
> —Eeya-Keen Healing Center Inc.

At first pass, it might seem as though this archetypal—but also intensely personal—reading of *The Shining* is at odds with the various interpretations found in *Room 237*. Actually, it is congruent with all of them—as befits an original myth, a psychological blueprint which, like time itself, is found underlying all human endeavors.

The more private, domestic dynamic of the broken father and the betrayed child is one that, since it describes a formational experience, would be expected to manifest on a macrocosmic level through any number of unconscious re-enactments of that primary wound. There is, like the Overlook Hotel, no getting away from it.

In *Room 237*, Geoffrey Cocks believes *The Shining* is about the Nazi genocide of the Jews. In a speech given in 2005, "The Childhood Origins of the Holocaust," Lloyd deMause convincingly traces the Nazi persecution of Jews back to the widespread abuse of children in Germany in the years leading up to the 1930s. Most of the men who grew up to be Nazis suffered traumatic childhoods.[63] While deMause makes clear the connection between child abuse and persecutory governmental policies, he doesn't specifically identify the element of paternal neglect or abuse. Nonetheless, it can be easily inferred, because even when a child is abused by the mother or another caregiver without the father's consent or participation, the abuse is only possible due to the absence or indifference of the father.

As deMause said in the same speech, "historically fathers were mainly missing during the child's early years." The father's role is not just disciplinary (which so easily becomes tyrannical and abusive), but that of protector. So "The vast majority of child physical and sexual abuse is committed in single-parent homes, homes usually where the father is not present."[64]

For his part, Bill Blakemore argues that *The Shining* is about a different holocaust: the genocide of the Native American peoples. At some level, this subtext is even consciously acknowledged by Kubrick, seeing as there's quite a bit of Native American imagery in the film, as well as a seemingly superfluous reference to the Overlook being built on a Native American burial ground (a horror movie trope that's absent from the book).

The Native Americans are the indigenous inhabitants of America—the "children" of the land. When the colonizers came in increasing numbers, they began to treat the Natives with contempt, or at best indifference: slaughtering them wantonly, on the one hand, making deals they never intended to keep, on the other. In Canada, they were viewed as children not just symbolically but legally: "First Nations were viewed as children or wards of the state, to which the government had *a paternalistic duty to protect and civilize* ... 'the legal status of Indians of Canada is that of minors with the Government as their guardians.'"[65]

Besides making Natives legally equivalent to children, the colonizing forces in Canada abducted Native children into residential schools, where abuse of every kind, including sexual, was the norm and where the mortality rate was as high as 50 percent. The similarity between the Canadian residential schools and Nazi death camps is only one of the parallels between US/Canadian and Nazi policy. And other regimes too: "The Indian Act was used as inspiration for policies of apartheid in South Africa and, some would say, Palestine, among others around the world," and US policy toward the Natives was referred to in 1867 as "the final solution."[66] In *Hitler and His Secret Partners*, James Pool traces Hitler's inspiration back to the American Wild West:

> Hitler liked to draw an example of mass murder from American history. He viewed the fighting between cowboys and Indians in racial terms. In many of his speeches he referred with admiration to the victory of the white race in settling the American continent and driving out the inferior peoples, the Indians ... He was very interested in the way the Indian population had rapidly declined due to epidemics and starvation when the United States government forced them to live on reservations. He recognized the American government's forced migrations of the Indians over great distances to barren reservation land as a deliberate policy of extermination.[67]

The inference is clear, "the terror that swept across America" (the seemingly incongruous tag line for *The Shining* when it first opened in the US) hadn't begun there. And it wouldn't end there either.

Juli Kearns's reading of *The Shining* (in *Room 237*) focuses on the maze aspect of the film and the many architectural anomalies in the construction of the Overlook film set. She relates it to the myth of the Minotaur on a rather tenuous (or to be kinder, intuitive) bit of evidence, that of a poster of a skier seen on the wall behind the Grady daughters (as well as, of course, the maze). Underneath the poster is the word "Monarch," which is not referred to in *Room 237* (Monarch = King).

The myth of the Minotaur concerns Minos, the son of the god Zeus and a mortal woman, Europa. The story begins with the death of Minos's adopted father, King Asterius, and Minos' attempt to assume the throne. When his right to rule is challenged, he claims it is a divine right. He prays to the god Poseidon and is sent a sacred white bull for a sacrifice. Minos gains the throne but tries to cheat the gods by keeping the bull for himself, sacrificing an ordinary bull in its place. Minos' wife is bewitched by the gods, disguises herself as a cow, and mates with the white bull, giving birth to the Minotaur. (His proper name was that of Minos's adopted father, Asterius, meaning "star" or "starry one"—the star child.) To hide the shame of the forbidden offspring, Minos builds a labyrinth and hides him inside it. Later, Minos attacks Athens and demands a yearly offering of seven young men and seven young women as sacrifices to the Minotaur.

Jeff Searle writes, "The lair of the Minotaur may have been as much a spiritual one—a dark and confusing place of the mind—as a physical construction ... a symbol of unreason ... The Greek word *labyrinthos* may derive from the pre-Greek *labrys*, referring to a double-headed axe which was the dominant religious symbol in Minoan civilization. The 'labyrinth' would therefore be the 'house of the double-headed axe.'"[68]

Minos was apparently twice refused his father's blessing: once by Zeus and then by his stepfather, Asterius, the proof being that his right to the throne was questioned. This set in motion the sequence of events that led to the birth of Asterius, Jr., the star child who becomes the monster.

The most elaborate of the *Room 237* interpretations is Jay Weidner's contention that *The Shining* was a concealed confession of Kubrick's secret involvement in faking the Apollo Moon landing footage. In many ways, this is the most compelling of the readings, but it's also the least symbolic and most literal-minded. Even so, the same archetypal narrative can easily be extracted.

The US government is here the corrupt father figure that "abuses" the "child," Kubrick. Whether it's done by tempting or coercing, or a bit of both, it leaves Stanley forever scarred by the betrayal. *"Never, ever go near power. Don't become friends with anyone who has real power. It's dangerous,"* said Kubrick. Considering the power Kubrick wielded in his life, from his mid-30s onward, he clearly wasn't talking about Hollywood studio execs. Nor was he talking about having a brush with power, but *becoming friends* with it. Kubrick may have been talking about the

US government—since that was the most likely kind of real power he formed an alliance with—but he might as well have been talking about his own father. He could also have been giving advice to Danny Torrance.

(It's also possible that King—as the father of the novel—was a stand-in for the paternal authority figure Kubrick was defying, whose blessing he made damn sure he would never get, by flaunting just how little he cared about getting it. If so, he was perfectly named: Stephen means "crown.")

Weidner's view is that Kubrick cut a deal with the US government, that in exchange for faking the Moon landing footage, he was given "absolute power" as a Hollywood filmmaker, a power that depended on total secrecy. When he broke the terms of the agreement, Weidner claims, someone close to him was killed. True or false, what Weidner is describing is a heavily conditional blessing. Kubrick would only enjoy the protection of the father as long as he was subservient *to* him.

Besides filicide, another way the corrupt king/fallen father prevents his male heir from ever replacing him is (as Cronos did to Uranus) by *castrating him*. If there's any truth in this reading at all, Kubrick would have been compromised—emasculated—in the worst way possible: as a father and husband. He would have been unable to protect his family. He would have lived in perpetual fear of becoming a man who killed his family by failing to save them.[69]

The symbolism of an illusory journey to the Moon is also telling: Moon being a symbol of the mother, as well as lunacy, deception, dreams, and psychism, all subjects of *The Shining*. A child who cannot trust in his father remains eternally bonded (psychically) to the mother.

Adult boy

> "Ye are of your father the devil, and the lusts of your father ye will do. He was a murderer from the beginning, and abode not in the truth, because there is no truth in him. When he speaketh a lie, he speaketh of his own: for he is a liar, and the father of it."
> —John 8:44

Last but not least, there's John Fell Ryan. In *Room 237*, though he doesn't offer an overarching reading, Ryan makes some acute observations about *The Shining* (such as that article about incest). His main contribution to

Room 237 is the inspiration he had of playing the film both forward and backward simultaneously. The obvious significance of this device is that it allows time—Cronos, the central character of the film, according to Kael—to run both forwards *and* backwards. This reverses the accepted understanding of causality: what appeared to be a cause becomes an effect, and vice versa. The father is the child of the man.

Like Danny's backward steps in the snowy maze, Ryan's device can be seen as a literalization of the attempt (usually semi-conscious, at best) to get free of ancestral sins. History repeats itself when we don't learn from the past: yet the repeating is an attempt *to* learn; the opportunity is always there to *reverse* the flow and undo the mistakes of the past. This two-way flow between father and son (cause and effect) makes them one psyche with two different sides or directions. For the son to individuate and free himself of the sins of the father—his unlived life—he must "undo" the past and break the paternal narrative, expose the cover-up.

Jack Torrance, in the book at least, is struggling to get free of an ancestral load, the "white man's burden." Jack takes the job at the Overlook in order to write, to individuate via self-examination (and to stay off booze). He is there to rediscover and reinvent himself by journeying into his unconscious, bringing the ghosts of the past to the light of consciousness. The unspoken goal of individuation is to integrate the many roaming entities of the id—to heal the psyche that has been shattered into a thousand pieces by the axe blow of the father. Besides Danny and Wendy (and to an extent Hallorann, though Jack never interacts with him until the moment he sticks his axe in him), everyone Jack encounters at the Overlook is an aspect of himself.

Jack is a man trying to "kill his family" in the *right* way—by slaying the familial spooks that possess him. When he fails—as a desperate, unconscious attempt to do it in a way that won't involve his own psychic annihilation—he becomes a man who *literally* tries to kill his family—in the wrong "direction." Instead of slaying the internal father, he tries to kill his son. History repeats.

One of the discoveries made as a result of the "obsessive" study of *The Shining* is that, among the many pages of Jack Torrance's manuscript (which Kubrick had a secretary type, every last page of), all consisting of the one line, "all work and no play make jack a dull boy," there is one page with the same typo repeated several times: "all work and no play make jack adult boy." (This whole scene is not in the novel.) Jack is *puer aeternus*, an "adult boy." He is a child who was never able to *be* a child, because his childhood was a battleground of lies and betrayals. The father's abuse and/or indifference forced him to grow up prematurely in order to survive. At the same time (like Peter Pan), it prevented him from ever maturing and kept him frozen at the age of original wounding. Because the child was unnaturally "adult," the adult became correspondingly infantile.

* * *

> "Most parents through most of history relate to their children ... as poison containers, receptacles into which they project disowned parts of their psyches."
> —Lloyd deMause, "Psychohistory: Childhood and the Emotional Life of Nations"

A foundational Bible myth of the Jews is that of Abraham, the Jewish patriarch, being ordered by Yahweh to sacrifice his son. This is Yahweh, later the God of Moses and the Ten Commandments, who created the Heaven and the Earth by His *word*. More locally speaking, "In the beginning was the word" pertains to the inception of written language and how this gave rise, not to just the possibility but to the *necessity* of an "I" behind the word. Both God and self are equally invisible, intangible entities who can be known only by the "words" (thoughts) that emanate from them. Yahweh couldn't be looked upon, and not even images were allowed to be made of Him; His only representative was the Word. Oddly enough, in the Gospel of John, the devil is also called "a liar and the father of it."

As Brian Rotman, among many others, has noted, there is a cultural war between text and image. This war rages on the inside as on the outside, a war between mind and body, or even mind and *psyche*: soul. "[T]he struggle between word and image has to be seen as carrying the 'fundamental contradictions of our culture' ..."[70] This war is neatly embodied in the *weltanschauungkrieg* (worldview warfare) between King and Kubrick (they even have the same initials). That King is a gentile and Kubrick a Jew inverts the cultural convention, since the Jews are the keepers of the word/text, a text which *forbids* the use of graven (or celluloid?) images.

The maze (central to the film but absent from the book) represents the neural pathways of right and left sides of the brain. It is both a parallel system (i.e., complete unto itself, like an image) and serial, i.e., a collection of linear pathways to be traversed and mapped, like a text.

Because words were the basis of the Jewish religion and culture, names are especially sacrosanct to it. In Kubrick's *The Shining*, both the father and the son are played by actors bearing the same names as their characters—Jack Torrance is played by Jack Nicholson, Danny Torrance by Danny Lloyd. Kubrick wasn't a practicing Jew, but he would have been aware how, in Judaism, the name of a person or thing is believed to give it its nature. What's more, the last name of the actor who plays Danny is shared by the phantom bartender who facilitates Jack's return to drinking: Lloyd.

Along with his sub-persona Tony, Danny's psychism—the shining—is at least partially the result of his having been abused, sexually or otherwise, by Jack. In the novel, there is no hint of sexual interference, but an incident in which Jack breaks his son's arm is an essential bit of backstory. This incident is referred to in the longer US version of the film (142 minutes), yet perversely, Kubrick cut the scene out, along with 20 minutes of far-from-superfluous footage, for the European version.

Kubrick's reasons appeared to have to do with the film's initially disappointing box office and reviews, but who knows? Perhaps he decided these scenes (and especially the one about Jack and Danny's history) provided too much of a human dimension to Jack and thence the film? At the same time, the film does suggest a sexual element to Jack's abuse of Danny, if obliquely. The scene in which Jack sits Danny on his lap in the bedroom is one of the darkest and most disturbing in the film; then there's that peculiar issue of *Playgirl*, with the incest story on the cover—something no viewer would ever have spotted before the days of DVDs and digital enhancements.

Some interpretations of Kubrick's *The Shining* have suggested that Jack also possesses the ability to shine and that he's in denial about it.[71] One I found claimed that Danny *uses* his power to bring Hallorann to the Overlook so he can be sacrificed in place of himself, Danny. One of Pauline Kael's many criticisms of the film was how much time it took getting Hallorann up to the Overlook simply in order to kill him: "The awful suspicion pops into mind that since we don't want to see Wendy or Danny hurt and there's nobody else alive around for Jack to get at, he's given the black man."[72]

There may be more truth to this than Kael suspected. As the black man, or shadow, Hallorann is the traditional *scapegoat*. The Overlook, like Yahweh, doesn't require the father to actually kill his son, only to prove his obedience via the harshest test of all. For Yahweh, any blood will do. (The idea of blood sacrifice is emphasized in the film by the choice of dates, as previously mentioned.)

More prosaically, Hallorann's arrival does serve to save Wendy at a crucial moment—the moment in which Jack breaks through the door and announces his arrival (in imitation of a famous talk show host). If Hallorann was chosen by Danny to die, it may be because he is a stand-in for the father who betrayed him. Hallorann lied to Danny when he said, "There ain't *nothing* in Room 237!" and he left him to his fate by abandoning him at the Overlook, knowing what he did about the place. Not that this makes him fit for execution, necessarily. But a child's unconscious "reasoning" can be more ruthless than a despot's.

Meanwhile, poor Jack tries but cannot individuate. He is stuck on a single line, repeating it endlessly: the "commandment" or program that has been installed into him, to work and not to play, to become dull. While he pounds out the same words, day after day, Danny thinks in images. When Danny uses words, it is not even in his own voice (which has been stolen from him by abuse) but that of "Tony," the demon installed into him by his father's rage and alcoholism. Tony is Danny's alter but also Jack's disowned "psychism," his poison. In the book, we find out toward the end that Tony is Danny's middle name, a concealed part of himself. And Tony has such distrust of words that he prefers to speak backward. (REDRUM.)

So far as the relationship between child abuse and psychic abilities goes, this is a thorny question, bringing together as it does two controversial subjects, both of which are regarded with skepticism from some quarters *independently*, never mind together. The "missing link" here may be what's been called schizophrenia (as well as autism and other anomalous perceptual conditions that have been diagnosed without ever being properly understood). The link between child abuse and schizophrenia is fairly well-documented, and that between schizophrenia and visions, apparent telepathic experiences, precognition, and the like ("psychism") is also well-known.

At first pass, this might seem almost like a side-topic, but in fact it's probably the axis around which the whole Kubrickon, as well as the Overlook, turns—as well as all of my previous "exegeses" (on Whitley Strieber especially). It's the soul of the plot, the self-same spot to which the circle ever returneth in. The original wound.

Jack's demon is his alcoholism, inherited from his abusive father. (Danny inherited it too, though not until Stephen King wrote *Dr. Sleep*, 30 years later.) By interfering with Danny—violating him both psychically and physically—Jack passes the demon into Danny, an endlessly repeating cycle which Kubrick indicates with the final image of *The Shining*.

In deMause's terms, Danny is Jack's *poison container*. He goes to the Overlook—itself a great, generational wound in search of psyches to possess—seeking to exorcise those demons. As the demons take him over instead, Danny becomes the necessary receptacle for Jack's impotent rage. The only way to offload the terrible psychic burden, to get free of the poisons eating him up from the inside, is to pass them on to the next generation.

The Shining is about the impossibility of moving forward as long as we are in the grip of the past. Danny walking backward out of the maze to escape his father. Abraham's descendants becoming sacrificial offerings to the Nazi State. Native Americans forced to become stand-ins for the childhood abuse of European colonizers. Kubrick's unholy allegiance to "power," by which he bought creative freedom, at the price of a heavily censored self-expression. The labyrinth of the Minotaur, the grandfather's "lusts" that eventually create a prison for the grandson. John Fell Ryan, whose life "turned into *The Shining*." All in varying ways show the dangers of allowing the past to define us, and how easily a home turns into a hell, and a maze becomes a death trap.

It's significant that the first manifestation of the demon that finally takes him over is when Jack breaks Danny's *arm* as a reaction to Danny interfering with Jack's *writing*. Writing is Jack's attempt (and King's, and Kubrick's) to individuate by taking ownership of *the word*. It is the means of his enslavement to the father's voice, via the conditional blessing that is a secret curse.

The voice, lest we forget, is a voice *in the head* (a shining). The obedience is that of a father who, like Abraham, consents to murder his own son.

The secret ally

"Stanley Kubrick was like the coldest guy in the Universe."
—Stephen King

A psychic child is the "driver" inside the hard drive of time.

In 2013, I spent many months researching, writing, and podcasting about the author and alleged "alien abductee" Whitley Strieber. I gave specific attention to experiments that Strieber claims were conducted on him, as a child, as part of a covert US intelligence program. These experiments involved inducing trauma and dissociation in the child Strieber's psyche, via extreme forms of abuse.

The aim of these experiments is difficult to say for sure, but one apparent effect (whether or not it was intended) was that young Whitley's psyche became unusually open to unknown psychic phenomena, including congress with seemingly non-human, possibly non-physical, entities. Strieber's work as an adult (from the time he began to have memories of this "alien" congress) has included a disturbing, pseudo-scientific, evolutionist belief that, through the psychic distress brought about by trauma (especially in childhood), a human being can develop unusual psychic abilities.

Before he began to write about his "real-life" memories of alien and government-induced trauma and psychism, Whitley Strieber was an author very much in the range and style of Stephen King (i.e., pulp horror fiction). The main difference between them is not the subject matter they write about or even the style of their writing, but that, unlike King, Strieber eventually began publishing his stories as *non-fiction*. Yet both writers present the idea that the fragmentation of the psyche—Strieber's in his own reported childhood experience, Danny's in King's fictional account—is like the splitting of the atom, with the child's psyche in place of the atom. I imagine Jung would have agreed. Kubrick read Jung quite closely, and *The Red Book* is mysteriously seen on Ullman's desk in the opening interview scene—most mysteriously of all, considering it wasn't published until 2009! (Especially pertinent to this subtext of *The Shining* is Jung's interest in Kundalini energy and Eastern mysticism.)

If the energy released through Danny's trauma is the psychic equivalent of nuclear power, what does it fuel? It fuels a factory that provides vehicles of materialization for discarnate entities, spirits, demons, ghosts, and astral fragments and that opens corridors into infinite worlds. This energy is the stuff, not only that dreams are made of, but psychic reality too. In my father's house are many mansions … As Wendy realizes toward the end of the book, "in some unknown fashion it was Danny's shine that was powering [the Overlook], the way a battery powers the electrical equipment in a car ... the way a battery gets a car to start."

(The Overlook is a Bardo realm, liminal space, limbo. Like all substrata of reality, it requires psychic energy—belief—to keep its engine running, to give it form and substance. In myths, Lucifer's realm—the physical universe—was created via the premature splitting off from God the "Father," whereby the Son ventured forth into the world while *remaining merged with the Mother's psyche*—i.e., trapped in *mater*, or "fallen.")

* * *

"[T]he physical changes that make us human are the incarnations, so to speak, of the process of using words."
—Terence Deacon, *The Symbolic Species*

Much has been made of the many discrepancies between the book and the film of *The Shining* and how, if looked at correctly, they create a map of Kubrick's intentions. Some say he didn't just alter the meanings, he *inverted* them (or *almost* inverted them, switching red for yellow rather than red for green, in the case of the Volkswagen car).

The film is certainly a puzzling artifact in comparison to the novel. On the one hand, it rips the book's heart and soul out, keeping only the body, the structure. On the other hand, it brings coherence to the story and elevates pulp to the level of fable or myth. It has an archetypal resonance that is perhaps (potentially) even more affecting than the groping pathos of King's novel, not *despite* but *because of* how Kubrick stripped its main character of just about every last recognizably human quality. I suspect this was an instinctive, preconscious process for Kubrick, one that he *became* conscious of in the midst of writing (or even making) the film, and that he began to do more and more consciously the more aware he became of it. I think it reflects the natural tension between the archetypal realm and the human one.

And the friction between the word and the image.

Whatever the case, one of the most notable differences (unremarked upon in *Room 237*) is how, toward the end of the film, Danny dissociates completely and Tony takes over. Tony replaces Danny's voice with his own. In the book, though Danny does dissociate toward the end and escapes into his interiority, the suggestion at an earlier point is that Tony is being integrated into Danny's psyche now that his use has outlived itself.

Tony represents the dissociated self, the "demon" that Jack put into Danny (possibly when he broke his arm). He certainly isn't a benevolent presence in the book or the film. Tony represents the programmed "I" that takes over Danny's consciousness when things get too awful for Danny to cope and when Danny gives up (to) the ghost. Danny never speaks again in the movie after this point, except at the very end. As he is escaping the maze, leaving his father to his bleak midwinter fate, he cries out, "Mommy!" and is reunited with Wendy.

Watching the scene, for the first time ever, I was emotionally overwhelmed by a moment in a Kubrick film. I understood the meaning of the scene in a flash, and it devastated me. Danny was returning to the safety of the mother's psyche (the second womb). He would never leave it now. The natural and necessary rite of passage had not only been interrupted, it had been hideously inverted. His father had turned into a big bad wolf and regressed to an ape-man.

No matter how much relief it provides for the viewer, Danny's reunion with Wendy can't be mistaken for a happy ending. It unfolds to the sound of the father's inchoate howling, as he limps helplessly to his death inside the icy labyrinth. We are seeing both effect and cause, cause and effect. Danny's return to the mother's psychic embrace is the outcome of his father's descent into madness and of his terrible brutality. But the reverse is also true: Jack's reduction to an empty, monstrous shell is the final result of remaining psychically bonded to his own mother. It doesn't matter how many times he checks out; he can never leave. The psyche that cannot move forward can only regress.

In the light of all these discoveries, it seems likely that the question of what a mother-bonded psyche *is* and how it can be "tapped" (like Danny is tapped by the Overlook), is the "silver key" to the Kubrickon.

Danny's psyche isn't just a fuel source, obviously; or rather, the fuel he provides—psychic energy—isn't just to power the hard drive of the Overlook but also to run it, as a driver runs a PC. Like the sleeping pod-people of *The Matrix*, Danny's psyche not only fuels the machine but also, via the psychic material of his sleeping/dissociated mind, provides *the raw data* to create and maintain the dream-world that keeps all its "guests" asleep.

Danny's psychism is sourced in his wound. His dissociated state is a waking dream-world (matrix), populated by the projected phantoms of his own fractured unconscious. The wound of the father's axe blow is ancestral, so naturally the *traumnovelle* (dream-story) it generates ripples down through the generations, creating fractals in time, a history of trauma repeating. Like the mansion in *Eyes Wide Shut* that is a receiver-transmitter for the sterile, hygienic sex fantasies of Dr. Bill, the Overlook is a blank screen onto which the action is projected by Danny's own interior "shine."

The matrix is the externalized womb. A mother-bonded psyche (male or female, but with special emphasis on the male) is a psyche without boundaries, a disembodied psyche. Since it remains half in and half out of the waters of the mother (the womb/psyche), it can't ever enter all the way into physical, embodied, individuated existence, and is forever in search of a home. This kind of psyche is easy to poach. Desperate for some sort of structure and stability, it is easy to lure into a false form of embodiment. It lacks the ground—the clear sense of its own boundaries—to know where the self begins and the world leaves off, to distinguish between fantasy and reality, dream and waking. This makes it easily led and easily lured into false realities.

Did Stanley Kubrick seek to become the Architect, the false father, the demiurge who would lure a legion of followers through a stargate of his own making, into the labyrinth, the Bardo realm of his cinematic architecture, and by bonding his audience to a sound and image "machine," make it sentient, *animate* it? (By "it," I was referring to the machine, though it could also refer to the audience.) Maybe, like Ozymandias, his aim was to save the world, and the best I can achieve by writing this, like Rorschach with his diary, is to fail to prevent him from doing so. But of course, I don't really believe that. Kubrick is Jack Torrance. The dedicated Kubraphile—the son of Kubrick—is Danny, the child who shines, who sees what others can't see. And the Kubrickon, naturally, is the Overlook. The ancient structure that contains it all, that wants to live by possessing the souls that enter.

So what about Wendy? Wendy is the secret ally of the Overlook, without whom none of it would be possible. Her complicity goes so deep it's invisible to everyone, most of all to Wendy herself. Just as the technology that most effectively infiltrates society—and possesses human consciousness—leaves no traces, she is the invisible mother who binds it all together. The Overlook isn't interested in Wendy because the Overlook *is* Wendy, and vice versa. And so, of course, she wins in the end.

Of course, this is only so because Wendy is also a non-individuated soul—whether mother- or father-bonded or both. Kubrick was (perhaps unconsciously) underlining this when he reduced Shelly Duvall's role to little more than a whimpering *victim*. As the wife of an alcoholic, Wendy is a *codependent type*, a counseling term that relates to borderline personality disorder and weak central cohesion, i.e., to having a shaky and undefined sense of self.

While working on this part of the book, I was curious enough to read *Dr. Sleep* (Stephen King's 2013 sequel to *The Shining*). Though a very enjoyable read, I didn't find any special clues to support my reading, except for one. On the first page of Chapter 8, "Abra's Theory of Relativity," a fully grown Danny remembers being a teenager, asking his mother why she never dated other men.

"One man was enough for me, Danny," she tells him. *"Besides, now I've got you."*

There's no indication, here or anywhere else in the book, that Wendy's statement is meant to chill us to the bone. Of course not. Trying to explain mother-enmeshment to the mother-enmeshed is like trying to describe a fish to a body of water (or sobriety to a spirit). It is an accepted part of the mother-enmeshed culture that mothers possess their sons "forever," until death and beyond. It is seen as a *good thing*.

Mothers are the original caretakers—they've always been here.

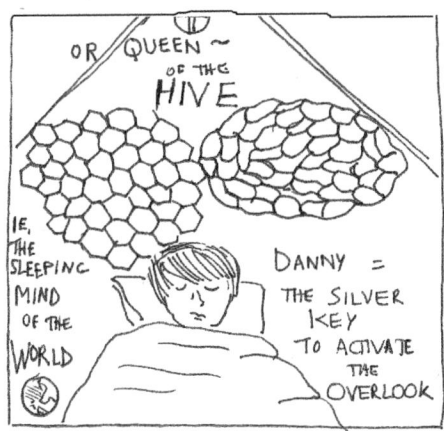

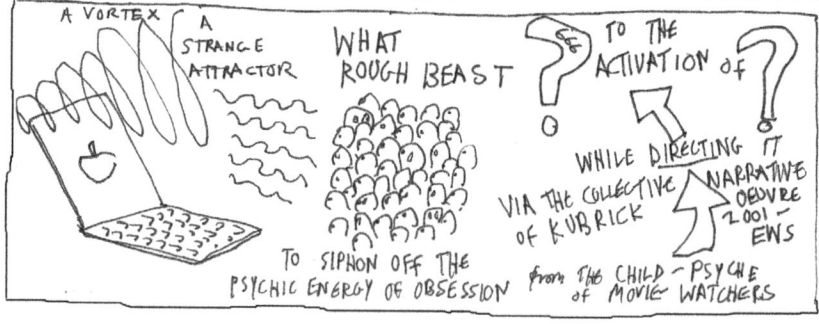

CHAPTER 9

Hive mind

"Beyond a certain point there is no return. This point has to be reached."

—Franz Kafka

The Rubicon is a shallow river in northeastern Italy just south of Ravenna, about 80 kilometers long. The Latin word *rubico* comes from the adjective *rubeus*, meaning "red." The river was so named because its waters are colored red by mud deposits. "Crossing the Rubicon" means to pass a point of no return. It refers to Julius Caesar's army crossing the river in 49 BC, which was considered an act of insurrection.

Rivers of blood, redrum, acts of insurrection. This was all decided long ago. *Alea iacta est*—the die is cast. (The Rubicon is perhaps best known as the place where Julius Caesar uttered this famous phrase.)

The Kubrickon is one in a series of explorations of public figures (Sam Peckinpah, Carlos Castaneda, Whitley Strieber, John de Ruiter, my brother, Aleister Crowley, Philip K. Dick, Roman Polanski). It's also the first time I have chosen one—had him thrust upon me—who was never really an influence, and certainly not a mentor or a guru. In all previous cases (Dick a partial exception), the men I wrote about were father/brother figures whose blessing I wanted, in one form or another, but couldn't get, and so got busy uncovering all the ways they were *unworthy* to bless me. In contrast to these figures, I never wanted anything from Kubrick.

In *The Shining*, Jack Torrance ends up possessed by the soul of the Overlook and by the previous caretaker, who it turns out—incoherently—was Torrance all along. While working on part one of this book, dreaming of the Overlook, I began to notice that I was acting more and more strangely. I was playing games, dangling clues in front of people, testing who was paying attention, thinking strategically, seeing the world and others as opponents on a kind of psychological chess board. In terms of real-world status and accomplishments, compared to Kubrick I was a mosquito on a Monolith. But then, I was after a livelier game than Monoliths. Kubrick was only the means to an end.

When you enter a paradigm with something that has the power to change the paradigm, by definition, the paradigm-changing element does not "exist" within the paradigm it is about to change. If it did, it would have no power to change it. Everything I say about Kubrick from within the Kubrickon gets turned into Kubrickanalia. Jack Torrance (the Kubrick-obsessive) can only see his own projections. By entering the dream of Kubrick's followers, I become an element of that dreamscape. I can say "This is all a dream" as many times as I want. But who will listen? My insistence may only make the dream more compelling.

In the process of trying to map the maze, am I becoming lost in it—like a detective who checks into the Overlook to investigate a murder and winds up committing one?

Word vs image

"Leaving language aside for the moment, which properly speaking is a bio-cultural given rather than a technological medium, the chief mind-constituting technology, 'mind-upgrade' … and the mother of almost all subsequent cognitive upgrades is writing. Writing in its two dimensions: the writing of ideas, patterns, and procedures whose most focused and abstract realization is the symbolic ecology of mathematical thought, and writing as an apparatus for inscribing human speech and thought among whose multiform achievements is the production of a literature and of a literate form of discourse that enables one to

> read and write texts—such as the present essay—about the nature of writing."
>
> —Brian Rotman, *Becoming Beside Ourselves*

Steven Shaviro wrote a book called *The Cinematic Body*, in which he wrote, "The text is the postmodern equivalent of the soul." Language is both biological and cultural, but writing is a form of technology. As such, it constitutes the most significant change to human consciousness that we know of. Writing has two functions: formulating entirely abstract concepts such as mathematics and representing human speech and thought, i.e., literature, including literature about literature, writing about writing.

Where all this pertains to AI and the Kubrickon is in the way digital media is the first technology to equal writing in its inevitable impact on human consciousness. Brian Rotman's premise is simple but radical: that the existence of an "I," a self-aware self (if that's not a total tautology), is possible only as the result of developing the technology of writing. The new digital technology heralds a whole new phase for human consciousness—as radical, by implication, as the difference between apes and men. The pen is mightier than the bone.

Now take a deep breath. Rotman's original hyper-thesis is that an irrevocable change is happening to the individual self (that's you). The thing that is thought to be most fundamentally fixed and final about human existence—our sense of being an individual, separate self—is becoming "unmoored as the technological upheaval transforming the landscape of Western culture makes itself felt deep within our heads, within our subjectivities, our personas, our psyches."[73] (Rotman, p. 81) (Liminal times, baby.) All the many myriad ways in which we connect to one another via technology, and both share and shape—shape *by* sharing—our experience of ourselves and each other, are "installing a new psyche at the cultural intersection" where technology and biology meet (Ibid).

What rough beast is slouching toward Babylon?

Consider the ape at the start of *2001*. Did some internal change occur which caused the ape to pick up the bone, or did picking up the bone allow for a change in the ape's experience of itself and its environment, leading to a corresponding cognitive shift within its psyche? Clearly, it was both.

(I'm going to leave the Monolith out of the equation—though it's kind of irresistible to note how it's been compared to the modern tablet computer and smartphone. As I edit this chapter, I am sitting on the London overground heading for Willesden Junction. On either side of me are women and men in communion with their smartphones. Roughly half the people on the carriage are doing the same. No one besides me is reading a book, which means *I* am the weirdo here. Future humans will probably have extra-large and hyper-flexible thumbs.)

Technology makes new kinds of behavior and social interaction possible and even necessary. It emphasizes some modes of activity and suppresses others; it draws us into repeating certain patterns of action and avoiding others. This is how "technological media constitute and reshape psyches in particular, medium-specific, directions" (Rotman, pp. 82–83).

So far, so apocalyptic.

Rotman introduces the concept of two particular kinds of cognition, which he calls "the serial/parallel duo." Serial cognition relates to language, text, and ordinary thinking: it orders sense impressions (actions, events, etc.) into a linear sequence, one after the other, as in text on a page, narrative. The other form of cognition is parallel, that is, impressions that are received and stored side-by-side, simultaneously, as in an image in which all the elements co-exist, without any one of them obviously preceding or following the other. (This may be how we dream at night.) Basically: words and pictures require different modes of cognition.

There is a fundamental duality in everything. An obvious example is music, which requires both melody (hierarchy or linear sequence) and harmony (co-operation, co-existence). Rotman sees this duo as being "frequently the site of larger cultural and technical battles." He cites the well-known Biblical prohibition of graven images (while favoring grave texts!), and the Platonic distrust of imagery: "the history of culture [he writes] is in part the story of a protracted struggle for dominance between pictorial and linguistic signs, each claiming for itself certain proprietary rights on a 'nature' to which only it has access."

Simply put, who or what gets to define reality: word or image—Stephen King or Stanley Kubrick?

Games of thrones

> "The fourth industrial revolution, however, is not only about smart and connected machines and systems. Its scope is much wider. Occurring simultaneously are waves of further breakthroughs in areas ranging from gene sequencing to nanotechnology, from renewables to quantum computing. It is the fusion of these technologies and their interaction across the physical, digital and biological domains that make the fourth industrial revolution fundamentally different from previous revolutions."
> —Klaus Schwab, *The Fourth Industrial Revolution*

If memory and knowledge are the building blocks of identity, "the fundamental agents of change and structure," then the question of how exactly memory-knowledge is represented and stored is equally fundamental. The medium is the message. According to Rotman, not surprisingly, these two forms of cognition employ "entirely different neural mechanisms."

If all recorded history (whether in text or image) traces a seemingly endless struggle for dominance between these two modes of expression/experience, the reverse is also true, namely, that it is only via the co-existence, and the apparent competition, of these two modes that anything has ever been perceived to be happening at all! At the same time, the fact that history has been characterized primarily by succession dramas (games of thrones) may be a result of the seeming incompatibility—the inability to reach truce or synthesis—of these two modes of cognition. Digital media may herald—both symbolically and actually—just that magical synthesis. Rotman calls it "an enormous idea machine, a combinatorial technology that permits the signifying, patterning, imagining, constructing, and discovering of an apparently endless plenitude of entities" (Rotman, p. 86).

If "Computer architectures are ultimately abstractions of how we think about reality" (Norman Margolus), they are also the means by which we restructure or transform our internal cognitive and perceptual faculties, and so begin to experience reality in new ways.

Rotman points out how the interlinking of many different perceptual "nodes" in order to process and share information "is an intrinsic characteristic of most natural phenomena." He cites social organizations from honeybee colonies to modern corporations as "living examples of distributed information processing." "Computation in biological brains," he writes, "especially in their sensory processors such as vision systems, displays a high degree of distribution" (Chandrasekaran, quoted pp. 89–90). The behavior of crowds, workgroups, couples, families, theater audiences, and non-human collectives from slime molds, reefs, and colonies to every kind of flock and swarm, are all examples of a non-technology-dependent manifestation of this kind of collective intelligence.[74]

Alan Turing (most famous now for the Turing test: how to recognize artificial intelligence when we encounter it) was largely responsible for the commonly held idea of a computer as a linearly proceeding sequence of computational movements, matching what most of us still assume to be the workings of our minds, performing a chain of reasoning, or reckoning. In other words, linear, not parallel, processing. Edwin Hutchins referred to this as the "origin myth of cognitive science." In fact, it is impossible to separate the process of internal, linear thought from the environment in which it occurs, i.e., both the body of the individual and the circumstances that body is situated in. Simply put, the "computation" process of human consciousness *does not happen only in the mind but also in the body and the total environment*, about which the human is "computing." It is an interactive process.[75]

We think of our own intelligence as something individualistic and of thought as taking place inside our heads. But in order to maintain this idea, we have to see everything outside of that interior mind-self process as incidental, as mere context without any substantial role in the thinking process besides inspiring or informing it in some way. Rotman argues that this context is actually "a crucial element in how humans think; not only is thinking always socially and culturally placed and mediated through technology, but this is the only way it can happen." Simply put, we don't merely use language and image to think, language and image use us, and use thought, to propagate and/or experience *themselves*.

To understand the relationship between individual and collective intelligence, we have to first learn to distinguish between the "cognitive properties of the culture"—the collective consciousness matrix which we are plugged into—and those that are inherent to ourselves, as individuals "manipulating the elements of that system."

It is this relationship that parallel computing puts into flux. Our digital technology does not operate by the rules of "I," of individual linear thinking, but by those of "distributed bio-social phenomena," that is, collective thought processes and expressions that burst through the parameters of an isolated, individual self and render it, if not incoherent or impotent, as something entirely different than we had previously imagined it to be. The new technology is introducing into our *interior* lives "parallelist behavior," namely, knowledge and desires that complement and ultimately dissolve the idea of a single "I." We are becoming colonized by our technology. A species possessed.

This is the Hive Mind, and this is also the form of "AI" which Stanley Kubrick—in the employ of a highly secret think tank of supersophisticated philosophers, scientists, mathematicians, and computer programmers—was dedicated to bringing into operational existence. The Kubrickon.

Behold the para-self

> "Mediological recognitions of writing's formation of the self come (and perhaps could only come) at the close of its influence. We are now witnessing a displacement of the written text's hold on the self: a post-literate self is emerging, patterned not on the word—stable, integral, fixed, discrete, enclosing a unique interior meaning, ordered, sequential—but on the fluid and unordered multiplicities of the visual image."
> —Brian Rotman, *Becoming Beside Ourselves*

One recent and well-known example of a Hive Mind in action is the Anonymous phenomenon, which emerged out of the early, early internet message board subculture of 4chan (also known, with irony, as the Internet Hate Machine). While the repercussions of Anonymous activity extended quickly into the IRL/AFK (in real life, away from keyboard) world (for example, with the anti-Scientology demonstrations), such repercussions would not have been possible without prior organizing via the internet. That this was a natural, even predictable, evolution of the tech is confirmed by a message from one of the original creators of the internet, anonymously of course, on an online forum, enturbulation. org, in 2007. The thread was titled "From the Internet's Old Guard":

> I, like most of my friends, continued on in fields associated with technology and communications. We were all there creating ARPANET (the predecessor of today's Internet) ... working within the frameworks of the IEEE and other orgs to create what every-

one today enjoys as the Internet. We ran the first USENET servers. We collaboratively developed SMTP and e-mail. We designed, built and maintained the various IRC nets and servers ... What I'm trying to say is that the actions of Anonymous have GENUINELY captured the interest of a LOT of very highly placed people. We old-timers have fought a lot of battles. Most of them have been for stupid and personal or trivial reasons over the development of "internet" communications. What Anonymous (and EVERYONE who has joined in the fight against Scientology) has done lately ... well, that's a HUGELY different thing ... WE ARE FUCKING HUGELY BEHIND YOU. Every single peer I've talked to has said the same thing: WHY HAS IT TAKEN SO LONG FOR THIS FIGHT TO BEGIN? I only wish I could list the number of top-level vice-presidents, directors and senior managers I'm friends with at ISP's (who have had to deal with Scientology's persistent BS demands) that are THRILLED TO THEIR TITS that this fight has finally gelled. Don't let your guard down. Remain COMPLETELY anonymous. That is your biggest strength. That, and know that there are some people who have been in this shit for DECADES that are watching you, working WITH you, and have JOINED you behind the lines to protect you. WE are watching THEM do stupid shit, and are documenting it as best we can.

While this suggests there was some high-level support for Anonymous (out of a shared animosity for Scientology), the individuals involved in the movement—many at least, and as far as we know—had no prior knowledge of each other and didn't (necessarily) develop any personal relations, but came together to form a collective intelligence with a specific purpose, like bees in a hive (or even a slime mold).

This seemingly new form of intelligence was collective but also in a sense "artificial," insofar as it materialized into a recognizable form via technology. If Marshall McLuhan and Rotman are right, then the technology not only made the emerging intelligence possible, it informed it and used it as a vehicle of its own incarnation. AI. It is also consistent with postmodern accounts of human nature as *"consistently collectivist, holding that individuals' identities are constructed largely by the social-linguistic groups they are a part of."* (Hicks, pp. 6–7, emphasis in original).

What's more, where multiplicity meets intersectionality and identity becomes politics, *"postmodern themes in ethics and politics are characterized by an identification with and sympathy for the groups perceived to be oppressed in the conflicts, and a willingness to enter the fray on their behalf"* (Hicks, pp. 6–7, emphasis in original). The continuum within the Hive Mind is wide; it spans the gulf between the id monsters of 4chan's Internet Hate Machine (which, despite its primordial irreverence, first became IRL active in its pursuit of child molesters on the internet) and its shadowy sister in the super-egomania of social justice warfare and cancel culture, which uses hate not for the lulz, but in its perversely self-righteous war against intolerance. (Unspeakable memes of 4chan meet the virtue signals of the SJW!)

The way a Hive Mind thinks and acts is very different from how individual minds think and act, and correspondingly hard to predict, control, or counteract. It sees things that a single cognitive perception misses, just as a satellite image taken from thousands of feet above the ground sees things a city dweller can't. In the case of a collective "I," *both* perspectives are available, since a collective is also made up of individual perspectives. (Imagine multiple TV screens on a wall: you are able to watch all simultaneously, or focus on a single one.)

Rotman's premise is that via digital technology, "parallelism"—the ability to perceive many different aspects at once and form many different perspectives simultaneously—is being introduced into individual awareness and transforming the self into a multiplicity. At the same time, Rotman suggests that, as this happens, there is a subtle interface with a preexisting multiplicity, that of the cells of the body and the nervous system. As without, so within: the Hive Mind coming into existence via technology is a mirroring (or "aping")—and perhaps an inevitable development of—the *interior* collective intelligence of the body itself.

At present, our experience of an interior self is largely dictated by an internal dialogue that tells us—like the Terminator in the 1984 B-movie, with its drop-down menu inside its head (via an ongoing, ceaseless narrative) who we are, what's going on, how to feel and how to respond. Because this narrative is linear, it appears to emerge from a single source—the mind-self. With increasing reliance on the practical use of imagery (and touch, which Rotman points out is central to our experience of technology), the nature of the narrative is transforming into a post-textual, non-linear narrative with many different sources: a "multiple 'I'" whose locus is both inside the body and outside it, but that is certainly not confined to the mind, or what we have come to think of as the mind (which is little more than a constant stream of textual data). This both allows for and makes inevitable—the emergence of a new subjectivity.

The curious thing about digital imagery is that it is both image *and* text: code that creates image. So, far from being a throwback to a previous, more visual kind of bias (human pre-language consciousness), it is the fusion of two previously predominant perceptual modes into a *third thing* that transcends both. This fusion inevitably appears, from the current, dominant, serial-linear perspective at least, as a confrontation, a battle for dominance. Stephen King fighting with Stanley Kubrick over the definitive version of *The Shining*. Yet it is precisely when "a new medium confronts and absorbs its predecessor" that "communicational media can facilitate new psychic entities and objects of belief" (Rotman, p. 107). (Ghosts inside the Overlook.) Rotman's para-self is born, like nuclear power, "from a process that reaches down to the level of the image's atomic structure."[76]

Is that where the demonically driven *Shining* exegetists are trying to get to?

DID Meets DOD: the AI breakthrough

> "Once, not so long ago, there was an absolute separation of self and other: an 'I,' identical to itself as an autonomous, indivisible, interior psyche opposed to an external, amorphous collectivity of third persons outside the skin. Now the 'I'/'me' unit is dissolving, the one who says or who writes 'I' is no longer a singular, integrated whole but multiple, a shifting plurality of distributed I-effects, I-roles, I-functions, and I-presences. Now the 'I' bleeds outwards into the collective, which in turn introjects, insinuates, and internalizes itself within the 'me': what was private and interior is seen as a fold in the public, the historical, the social as outside events enter (and reveal themselves as having always entered) the individual soul in the mode of personal destiny."
>
> —Brian Rotman, *Becoming Beside Ourselves*

In perhaps the most shocking predestined collision of them all, Rotman compares the para-self to the modern diagnosis of *dissociative identity disorder*, or DID. He also mentions the known link between it and childhood abuse. And so we are back at the place we never left, the Overlook Hotel, where child abuse, dissociative identity disorder, psychic entities, and an emerging para-self (the shining) intertwine into a maze of as-yet unfathomed meanings.

The difference, Rotman argues, between DID sufferers and the rest of us is that, in the first case, there is no single coherent representation of a self to which the person can attribute the many interior processes (voices, etc.), so the person experiences them as the thoughts, perceptions, and expressions of a variety of different entities (like Jack Torrance encountering the ghosts of Lloyd and Grady). When our sense of a single representation of self is coherent and clear, the same conscious processes can be attributed to a single "I." In both cases, a multiplicity is really at work.[77]

To diverge briefly back into the quagmire of identity politics, there is currently a booming dissociative identity disorder community traceable online, for example, inside the Chinese company TikTok, where "Influencers who say they have DID, once known as multiple personality disorder, are a vocal—and controversial—presence on the app." One such "influencer collective" is described as one of many members of a 29-person system, "all of whom share a single body, brain, and life. Each person, or 'alter,' in the system is a distinct form of consciousness [all of which] live together in the body of a 31-year-old man diagnosed with dissociative identity disorder (DID)."[78] To create a singular identity out of the multiplicity of DID is another example (after the 4chan to SJW curve) of how a cellular id-awakening is co-opted and quashed by the tyrannical entity-intervention of the superego.

In Nature, there are certain kinds of insects that group together into a specific formation, so they appear from above to be a single, larger creature, thereby avoiding being picked off by predators. The group formation is a kind of defensive posture of the collective that temporarily forms what might be called an imaginary "I." The "I" self of human beings is similar to this defense posture, except for one key difference: in human beings, the defensive "I" has become fixed (due to early trauma) and cannot easily return to its constituent parts, like a face that has got stuck into a single expression.

When this happens, the multiple nodes of consciousness can no longer function as nodes (or even as conscious in any true sense), because they are committed (by the imagined threat of outside attack) to maintaining an illusory façade of individuality. This larger, imaginary "I" is ineffective *except* as a defense. The "bugs" can't go about their business when they are huddled together in such a limited arrangement; ditto the multiplicity of consciousness in a human being.

The dissolving of the imaginary "I" self would, of course, be experienced (in the initial stages) as a kind of shattering annihilation, because it brings an end to the arrangement which created the illusion of its existence. Yet nothing of consciousness is actually destroyed. Consciousness is only released from the bondage of an illusory position. It continues, only now as a multiplicity of "personalities" all working together. DID is the result of an only partial dispelling of the illusion, in which the *idea* of a single, presiding I-self remains, even while the fragmentations occur. The experience is then not of intimately associated parts returning to a harmonic working relationship but of conflicting fragments rubbing up against each other and vying for dominance.

In the bug analogy, the fact the bugs are able to organize themselves into an arrangement that successfully creates the illusion (to predators, note, not to themselves!) that they are in fact a single, larger, united organism indicates that, even when they disperse and continue on their way in an apparently independent fashion as "individuals," they are still part of a collective subjectivity. The same must be true of the human "I" of an ego self. It is an imitation (a poor one, designed only for a single purpose, that of protection/defense) of *a deeper kind of unity and cohesion* that is not dependent on any kind of "huddling." It is potentially the means for a distributed, multiple, parallelist (multi-locational) form of activity.

Rotman's point is that the prevalence of technological mediation (like computing and digital imaging) may be engendering specific types of behaviors and thereby reconfiguring both our cognitive and our perceptual faculties; but it's only *the preexistence of an internal "multiplicity of subjects"* that allows a new pluralized self, or para-self, to come into being.[79]

* * *

"Part of the AI breakthrough lies in the incredible avalanche of collected data about our world, which provides the schooling that AIs need. Massive databases, self-tracking, web cookies, online footprints, terabytes of storage, decades of search results, Wikipedia, and the entire digital universe became the teachers making AI smart."
—Kevin Kelly, "The Three Breakthroughs That Have Finally Unleashed AI on the World" (*Wired*, October 2014)

Whether or not Stanley Kubrick ever read Brian Rotman (whose background was not in computing but in theater), what we do know is that, with the help of Arthur C. Clarke, he created his own prophecy of artificial intelligence in what became the most highly respected and "authentic" science fiction film ever made. Kubrick anticipated that the conventional way to create AI—to create a computer intelligent enough to make decisions, learn, respond, play chess, and have a rudimentary understanding of emotion, without actually being *sentient*—would inevitably lead to the *2001* scenario in which HAL decides that human beings are too unpredictable, threaten to interfere with the mission, and must be eliminated.

Kubrick and Clarke were, I think, correct in deducing that this would be the inevitable, logical conclusion of a super-computer able to calculate and make decisions based *exclusively on data* and not on any kind of empathic ability to relate, either to the environment or to other forms of sentient life. (HAL is an artificial forerunner to the sociopathic Alex.) The logical way to prevent this eventuality, Kubrick reasoned, would be to create machine intelligence that *could* relate to human beings in a sentient manner, that could recognize them as a fellow form of life and not just a problem to be solved. Only what has life can respect, or even recognize, other life forms.

According to *Wire* magazine's 2014 update on the progress of AI technology, one of the three necessities for the creation of AI is a large enough data bank for the machine to "learn" from. Kubrick would have known this; he also would have known that it wasn't only the *quantity* of information but also the *quality*. To this end, he may have set about to create a necessary *foundation* for a future database, to consist of *a particular kind of data*, information characterized by its intensely *subjective* nature, information that would effectively be "alive"—in constant flux—and not just fixed, lifeless information.

His films were increasingly designed in this way, to be effectively unfinished, conspicuously lacking—more like *ideas of films* than films themselves. Because of this unfinished quality, lacking coherence, unconscious content, recognizable human emotions, dramatic arcs, and so forth, his films not only invite but *demand* imaginative engagement: *they are not artistic solutions but scientific problems*. By stripping them of art, while at the same time presenting them (via his own ever-increasing status as a creative genius) as the *sine qua non* of art, he invoked the artist in the ordinary observer.

Countless exegeses on *The Shining* are filled to the brim with the more lifeless, objective kind of information: minutiae covering every shot, camera angle, micro-second mark, and so on. But the context for all of this data-gathering is that of the more sentient, imagination-fueled, ultra-subjective kind of perspective. As a result, we have objective data weirdly recontextualized by highly idiosyncratic, individualized interpretations. This kind of bizarre, obsessive, 100 percent *subjective* perspective can't be processed by a computer in the same way as raw data. In fact, it can't be processed at all *as* information. How do you file a "fact" that isn't based on any sort of empirical perception? How would a super-computer "decide" what *The Shining* is "really" "about," based on the information provided by *Room 237*?

For a computer to "understand" subjective data, it would first need to understand the nature of subjectivity. And this is only possible when there is a subject to understand it, i.e., *sentience*.

Theoretically and paradoxically, the machine becomes self-aware the moment it recognizes it lacks self-awareness. The awareness of the missing capacity creates *an opening* through which the new capacity can emerge.

> In this ongoing upheaval the old mono-self, the one-thing-at-a-time, linearly progressing lettered psyche with a sequentially orderable memory and a timeline history, is disappearing. Or rather, the hegemony, undisputed authority, and automatic intellectual and spiritual preeminence of such a writing-engendered monad is diminishing, giving way to a para-self, a parallelist extension of the "I" of alphabetic literacy that is crystalizing around us. And with it the conception of a single Truth and a singular notion of "truth," a single theory of the world, a single, all-encompassing deity, is become increasingly difficult to sustain.
>
> (Rotman, p. 133)

It is from this tension between text-based cognition and image-based perception, between the book and the film, between a single, fixed, empirical point of view and a multiple, moving, infinitely varying one, between subject and object, inner and outer, technology and biology, nature and artifice, *science and art*, that real sentience, both of the supposed human and the alleged machine, arises, *as a necessary guess*.

Perhaps this was even the originary cause of self-awareness, way back when, at the Dawn of Man.

BIBLIOGRAPHY

Arendt, Hannah (1958). *The Origins of Totalitarianism*. University of California.
Baudrillard, Jean (2001). *Selected Writings*. Stanford University Press.
Baxter, John (1997). *Kubrick*. New York: Carroll & Graf.
Benson, Michael (2018). *Space Odyssey: Stanley Kubrick, Arthur C. Clarke, and the Making of a Masterpiece*. New York: Simon and Schuster.
Bly, Robert (1990). *Iron John: A Book About Men*. Reading: Addison Wesley.
Clarke, Arthur C. (1961). *Challenge of the Spaceship*. New York: Ballantine Books.
Davis, Deborah (1979). *Katharine The Great: Katharine Graham and The Washington Post*. San Diego: Harcourt Brace Jovanovich.
Davis, Francis (2002). *Afterglow: A Last Conversation with Pauline Kael*. Cambridge: DaCapo.
Deacon, Terence (1998). *The Symbolic Species: The Co-evolution of Language and the Brain*. New York: W. W. Norton & Company.
Finn, Ed (2017). *What Algorithms Want: Imagination in the Age of Computing*. Cambridge: MIT Press.
Hicks, Stephen R.C. (2004). *Explaining Postmodernism: Skepticism and Socialism from Rousseau to Foucault*. Tempe: Scholargy Publishing.
Kael, Pauline (1970). *Kiss Kiss, Bang Bang*. London: Marion Boyars.
Kael, Pauline (1970). *Going Steady*. London: Marion Boyars.

Kael, Pauline (1975). *Deeper Into Movies*. London: Marion Boyars.
Kael, Pauline (1986). *Taking It All In*. London: Marion Boyars.
Kolker, Robert P. and Abrams, Nathan (2019). *Eyes Wide Shut: Stanley Kubrick and the Making of His Final Film*. Oxford: Oxford University Press.
Lethem, Jonathan (2012). *Talking Heads' Fear of Music* [33⅓ #86]. New York: Continuum.
LoBrutto, Vincent (1997). *Stanley Kubrick*. London: Faber and Faber.
Pool, James (1997). *Hitler and His Secret Partners*. New York: Simon & Schuster.
Rogak, Lisa (2008). *Haunted Heart: The Life and Times of Stephen King*. New York: St. Martin's Press.
Rotman, Brian (2008). *Becoming Beside Ourselves: The Alphabet, Ghosts, and Distributed Human Being*. Michigan: Duke University Press.
Saunders, Frances Stonor (1999). *Who Paid the Piper? The CIA and the Cultural Cold War*. London: Granta Books.
Schwab, Klaus (2018). *Shaping the Fourth Industrial Revolution*. London: Penguin.
Shaviro, Steven (1994). *The Cinematic Body*. University of Minnesota Press.
Snider, Steven William (unpublished). *The Secret History of Conspiratainment*.
Upton, Charles (2018). *Dugin Against Dugin: A Traditionalist Critique of the Fourth Political Theory*. Reviviscimus.
Wheen, Francis (2010). *Strange Days Indeed: The Golden Age of Paranoia*. London: HarperCollins.

ENDNOTES

1 From *Afterglow: A Last Conversation with Pauline Kael*, by Francis Davis, 2002, DaCapo, Cambridge.
2 Bill Harford is even less sympathetic a Kubrick protagonist than *The Shining*'s Jack Torrance. At least we feel for Jack's suffering (by the end at least). Cruise takes over the role of Harford because there is nothing there to fill out; it's the perfect role for a nothing presence like Cruise. Harford-Cruise is not just spineless and witless, a grinning fool, he is soulless, a mannequin in place of a man. There's absolutely nothing at stake in *Eyes Wide Shut*. Jack Torrance was an unpleasant and callous character, but we end up caring about him because of the depth of his suffering. Cruise's Harford doesn't suffer; he's not alive enough to suffer. He frets and pouts and then breaks down and cries. That's it.
3 Kubrick's insistence on endless takes "was the standard line that was being used to explain why Tom was no longer in touch with Miscavige, and it was not a very satisfactory answer to Miscavige. That was when he told Marty that his assignment in life was to get Tom Cruise back onboard." In the 2015 HBO documentary *Going Clear: Scientology and the Prison of Belief*, Rathbun maintains that he was assigned by Miscavige to "facilitate the breakup with Nicole Kidman." "How Nicole Kidman Almost Got Tom Cruise to Leave Scientology," by Marlow Stern,

Daily Beast, December 28, 2019: https://www.thedailybeast.com/how-nicole-kidman-almost-got-tom-cruise-to-leave-scientology

4   "Recall Stanley Kubrick's *Eyes Wide Shut* (1999): it is only Nicole Kidman's fantasy that truly is a fantasy, while Tom Cruise's fantasy is a reflexive fake, a desperate attempt to artificially recreate/reach the fantasy, a fantasising triggered by the traumatic encounter of the Other's fantasy, a desperate attempt to answer the enigma of the Other's fantasy: what was the fantasized scene/encounter that so deeply marked her? What Cruise does on his adventurous night is to go on a kind of window-shopping trip for fantasies: each situation in which he finds himself can be read as a realized fantasy—firstly the fantasy of being the object of the passionate love interest of his patient's daughter; then the fantasy of encountering a kind prostitute who doesn't even want money from him; then the encounter with the weird Serb (?) owner of the mask rental store who is also a pimp for his juvenile daughter; finally, the big orgy in the suburban villa. This accounts for the strangely subdued, statuesque, 'impotent' even, character of the scene of the orgy in which his adventure finds its culmination. What many a critic dismissed as the film's ridiculously aseptic and out-of-date depiction of the orgy works to its advantage, pointing towards the paralysis of the hero's 'capacity to fantasise.' This also accounts for the efficiency of the shot of Nicole Kidman sleeping, with the mask at her side, on her husband's pillow: in this version of 'death and the maiden,' she effectively 'steals his dreams,' being coupled with his mask, which stands for his fantasmatic spectral double. And, finally, this also fully vindicates the apparently vulgar conclusion of the film, when, after he confesses his nightly adventure to her, i.e. after they are both confronted with the excess of their fantasising, Kidman—upon ascertaining that now they are fully awakened, back into the day, and that, if not forever, at least for a long time, they will stay there, keeping the fantasy at bay—tells him that they must do something as soon as possible. 'What?' he asks, and her answer is: 'Fuck.' End of film, final credits. The nature of the *passage a l'acte* as the false exit, as the way to avoid confronting the horror of the fantasmatic netherworld, was never so abruptly stated in a film: far from providing them with a real-life bodily satisfaction that would render superfluous all empty fantasising, the passage to the act is rather presented as a stopgap, as a desperate preventive measure aimed at keeping at bay the spectral netherworld of fantasies. It is as if her message is: let's fuck as soon as possible *in order* to stifle the thriving fantasies, before they overwhelm us again. Lacan's quip about awakening into reality as an escape from the Real encountered in the dream holds more than anywhere apropos of the sexual act itself:

we do not dream about fucking when we are not able to do it—rather, we fuck in order to escape and stifle the excess of the dream that would otherwise overwhelm us." "*Eyes Wide Shut* and the Lacanian Real," by Slavoj Zizek: http://www.visual-memory.co.uk/amk/doc/0107.html

5   Davis, 2002, p. 112.
6   Cummings cites the video narration—erroneously—as being Michel Ciment's voice, because Ciment appears briefly at the start. In fact, it is Vachaud.
7   "Is *Eyes Wide Shut* a Requiem for Stanley Kubrick's Estranged Scientologist Daughter?" by Damien Leblanc, *Blouinartinfo*, August 8, 2013: https://web.archive.org/web/20180805203906/http://www.blouinartinfo.com/news/story/943711/is-eyes-wide-shut-a-requiem-for-stanley-kubricks-estranged
8   "The Secret of the Pyramid," by Laurence Vachaud, *Auticulture*, 2018: https://auticulture.com/the-secret-of-the-pyramid/
9   "Is *Eyes Wide Shut* a Requiem for Stanley Kubrick's Estranged Scientologist Daughter?" by Damien Leblanc, *Blouinartinfo*, August 8, 2013: https://web.archive.org/web/20180805203906/http://www.blouinartinfo.com/news/story/943711/is-eyes-wide-shut-a-requiem-for-stanley-kubricks-estranged
10 Another example of this academically *de rigueur* doublethink: Kolker and Abrams mock the "conspiracy theorists" who comb Kubrick's work for clues to support their theses, even going so far as to diagnose them as insane. One example they cite is (one I included in my summation of Vachaud's essay, which is not mentioned in Kolker and Abrams' book) of the two old men from Ziegler's party who reappear in the toy shop at the end. They put this down to Kubrick having to reuse extras and leave it there. Yet if this were so, it would be irrefutable evidence of Kubrick's sloppiness as a filmmaker, and specifically his *lack* of attention to detail, which is the very quality they adulate throughout the rest of their book, even over far more trivial examples, such as the color of a lamp shade.
11 See Benson, pp. 400–401. Kubrick forced Richter to choose between credit as an actor and as choreographer of the ape sequences. Richer chose actor credit.
12 "AMC Movie Guide's 50 Greatest Directors of All Time": https://www.imdb.com/list/ls008515415/
13 "The Greatest Directors In Movie History," *Ranker*, November 30, 2021: https://www.ranker.com/crowdranked-list/the-most-oscar-worthy-directors-of-all-time
14 With the exception of Juli Kearns in *Room 237*, all of the Kubrick exegetists are men. There are very few women captivated by his "genius."

I don't think I've even heard a female voice refer to Kubrick as a genius (though of course they are out there). The Kubrick cult is by and large a man cult.

15 "*Room 237*, Sundance 2012 Review," by Raffi Asdourian, January, 2012: https://thefilmstage.com/reviews/sundance-review-room-237/
16 Ibid.
17 "Stanley Kubrick Pal Dismisses *Room 237* Theories, Armond White Says Film Is 'End Of Cinephilia'" by Charlie Schmidlin, *IndieWire*, March 28, 2013: http://www.indiewire.com/2013/03/stanley-kubrick-pal-dismisses-room-237-theories-armond-white-says-film-is-end-of-cinephilia-100217/
18 Ibid.
19 "Stanley Kubrick's daughter debunks moon landing conspiracy theory," by Jacob Stolworthy, *The Independent*, July 6, 2016. http://www.independent.co.uk/arts-entertainment/films/news/stanley-kubrick-daughter-vivian-kubrick-apollo-11-moon-landing-conspiracy-theory-a7122186.html
20 Ibid.
21 Emphasis added. "The Genius of Stanley Kubrick and His Hidden Codes," *The Yellow Brick Road Free Blog*, April 11, 2014: https://web.archive.org/web/20170730153308/https://theyellowbrickroadfreeblog.wordpress.com/2014/04/11/the-genius-of-stanley-kubrick-and-his-hidden-codes/
22 http://www.sundance.tv/blog/2015/10/6-subliminal-secrets-hidden-in-the-shining
23 John Fell Ryan might agree. He claims that in *The Shining*, "At exactly 66 minutes and 6 seconds into the film, we cut from an image of the very devilish Lloyd the bartender to a shot of Jack taking his first drink, a drink he said he'd give his 'goddamn soul' for just a few minutes prior."
24 "Deep Blue Dreams: 666 Days of Stanley Kubrick," *They Know We Are Here*, July 25, 2015: http://debezoeker.tumblr.com/post/124994464036/deep-blue-dreams-666-days-of-stanley-kubrick
25 "*Eyes Wide Shut* and the Paranoid Style in American Pop Culture," *MoviePilot*, February 16, 2017: https://web.archive.org/web/20170216201949/https://moviepilot.com/p/eyes-wide-shut-paranoid-style-of-american-pop-culture/4208688
26 "*Room 237* reviewed by Armond White for *CityArts*," March 27, 2013: http://www.nyfcc.com/2013/03/room-237-reviewed-by-armond-white-for-cityarts/
27 Davis, Deborah (1979). *Katharine The Great: Katharine Graham and The Washington Post*. Harcourt Brace Jovanovich, pp. 137–138.

28 Davis (1979), p. 226.
29 Carl Bernstein, "CIA and the Media." *Rolling Stone* Magazine, October 20, 1977.
30 Since the first draft of this book, the author has amended this opinion, and I now see Nicholson's performance as effective *at its own level*, both as a kind of lampooning of the horror genre and a way not to be overwhelmed by the hysterical Gothic excess of Kubrick's effects—which include *how he directed Nicholson*. The overall effect of *The Shining* and of Nicholson's performance is a kind of *hyper*-reality—not so much dream reality, as some viewers have argued, or even the interior landscape of psychosis, but a movie-movie reality that makes it impossible for us to forget that we are watching a movie, and in many ways a rather unconvincing one (i.e., one that eschews the need for the usual kind of dramatic effects).
31 "Stanley Strangelove," *Deeper Into Movies*, p. 378.
32 As an easy example, Kubrick's later films seem to have been made by someone who doesn't really care for actors. A contentious statement, but one Robert Duvall—the actor, not Shelley Duvall's father, who is also named Robert—publicly expressed. "The actor called the work of Kubrick actors 'the worst performances I've ever seen in movies' and even went so far as to call the director an 'actor's enemy.'" "Robert Duvall Takes Aim at 'Actor's Enemy' Stanley Kubrick," http://67.20.55.118/2010/12/02/robert-duvall-takes-aim-at-actors-enemy-stanley-kubrick/
33 The story—the most interesting parts of it anyway—is more or less stolen from Nigel Kneale's terrific 1958 BBC mini-series, *Quatermass and the Pit*, in which an alien artifact is dug up and found to be evidence of humanity's distant ancestors and progenitors. *Childhood's End*, the Arthur C. Clarke book that most directly inspired the film, was "deeply rooted in the work of Olaf Stapledon" (Baxter, p. 204). Stapledon was a visionary, as every sci-fi aficionado knows, but his work is arguably best known as a result of being plagiarized by less talented writers like Clarke.
34 "A Clockwork Orange," *The International Anthony Burgess Foundation*: http://www.anthonyburgess.org/about-anthony-burgess/a-clockwork-orange
35 Bremer's diary, quoted in *Strange Days Indeed*, 2010 by Francis Wheen, p. 286.
36 To illustrate, try and imagine *The Shining* without a musical score and compare it to Hitchcock's *The Birds*, a film with no music at all. *The Shining* is almost totally dependent on its score to achieve its scare-effects. Judged as a horror movie, it has an almost deadening absence

of subtlety or finesse. This begins early on, with the first shot of the elevator gushing blood, a vision Danny has before the Torrance family have moved into the Overlook. With this insert, Kubrick breaks all the rules of the genre—and of intelligent filmmaking—hitting audiences with the most shocking imagery in the entire movie before it even means anything to us. He seems to be telling audiences, in the most ham-fisted manner: "Be afraid, damn you! Pay attention, *this is a scary movie and I am going to scare you!*" Only the most inept horror filmmaker would resort to this kind of tactic because it actually has the opposite effect: it puts audiences on guard and desensitizes them. Since Kubrick is not an inept filmmaker, this indicates that he is attempting to do something other than scare us.

37 "Why Do They All Say 'I'm Spartacus'? Meaning of the Movie Line," *Entertainment*, October 6, 2020: https://groovyhistory.com/im-spartacus-movie-line

38 "Researchers from the University of Melbourne achieved the feat by inserting electrodes through the jugular vein in the neck and pushing them up to the brain's primary motor cortex. Once there, the electrodes were nestled into the wall of the blood vessel where they could detect brain signals and feed them back to a computer." "Scientists discover new way to connect human brains to computers—through veins," Anthony Cuthbertson, the *Independent*, November 3, 2020: https://www.independent.co.uk/life-style/gadgets-and-tech/brain-computer-interface-vein-als-stent-neuralink-b1556167.html

39 Compare to: "Burgess always wanted to be seen as smarter than everyone—when readers pointed out to the master the mistakes in his magnum opus *Earthly Powers*, Burgess claimed he had deliberately included these errors to see who would discover them, which is like ye olde Thelwell cartoon of the riding instructor who when thrown by his horse, asked his pupils, 'Which one of you spotted my deliberate mistake?'" "Anthony Burgess and the Top Secret Code In *A Clockwork Orange*," by Paul Gallagher, *Dangerous Minds*, August 8, 2013: http://dangerousminds.net/comments/anthony_burgess_and_the_top_secret_code_in_a_clockwork_orange

40 "The brain makes files based on information it is given, usually through our senses but sometimes through our thoughts. If we have a sweetheart, being in the same room will give us that warm, romantic feeling. However, looking at their picture and thinking about them will do the same thing—even though they are not present. Even better, simply thinking about them will produce the same feelings (pulling the same file). The brain only reacts to the file or image, it doesn't care how it receives that image or information, by physical presence, by reminders

(pictures), or by 'thought.' Psychologists at the University of Chicago took three groups of basketball players. Group One practiced foul shots each day for thirty days. Group Two was instructed to 'imagine' shooting foul shots each day for thirty days. Group Three was instructed to do nothing. When tested, Group One (practicing shots) improved 24 percent. Group Three (doing nothing) had no improvement. Group Two, the group that only imagined shooting foul shots, improved 23 percent, yet did not physically touch a basketball. Why? As far as the brain knew, both groups that practiced (real and imagined) had shot foul shots daily, but Group Two never missed! Group Two, never missing, was given more emotional confidence by their brain and the brain also memorized the foul-shooting pattern as though they were on the court. In Group One, their brain experienced the hit-and-miss pattern of actual foul shooting which did not build confidence. Why mention this? We have the ability to build our own files, even when the actual real-world experience is lacking. Using our imagination, we can alter files by imagining new information." "Emotional Memory Management: Positive Control Over Your Memory, Page 4," by Dr Joseph M Carver, *Counselling Resource*: http://counsellingresource.com/lib/therapy/self-help/emotional-memory/4/

41 Brian Aldiss (author of *AI*) described Kubrick as "schizoid ... For Kubrick, it's 'I film, therefore I am.'" (Baxter, p. 44.) If his identity was wholly invested in the films he made, that alone might account for his need to exercise maximum control over how they were perceived by others.

42 See "The Mysterious Sri Lankan World of Arthur C. Clarke," *The Independent*, February 2, 1998. www.independent.co.uk/news/the-mysterious-sri-lankan-world-of-arthur-c-clarke-1142640.html. On one occasion, Clarke said of pedophilia: "I think most of the damage comes from the fuss made by hysterical parents afterwards. If the kids don't mind, fair enough ... There are two different definitions [of pedophilia], anyone who interferes with young boys who are not old enough to know their own minds and that's my definition. It varies for me." "Prince Charles, Arthur C. Clarke and the Paedophile Connection," *The Coleman Experience*, April, 2013. https://thecolemanexperience.wordpress.com/2013/04/27/prince-charles-arthur-c-clarke-and-the-paedophile-connection/

43 Arthur C. Clarke, "Proselytizer of Space," by Andrew Liptak, January 30, 2014. https://www.kirkusreviews.com/features/arthur-c-clarke-proselytizer-space/

44 "It is a strange thing that people who were interested in interplanetary travel were not necessarily interested in Science Fiction; more credibly those who were interested in Science Fiction were interested in

interplanetary travel, and thus, like spaceships gravitating towards a Black Hole they came to me as Hon. Secretary of the newly-formed Society: Arthur C. Clarke, Eric Frank Russell, Walter Gillings, Edward John Carnell, G. Ken Chapman, and William F. Temple ... Of course, it was I who went to P. E. Cleator as it happened, but the remainder gravitated to the fold. It appears that what I had started, more than an interplanetary society, was a Science Fiction movement. I had unwittingly succeeded where in 1931 Walter and myself had failed." "THEN By Rob Hansen—Chapter 1: The 1930s: GENESIS." http://fanac.org/Fan_Histories/Then/Then_11.html

45   This is from "Creating a Self-Fulfilling Prophecy" a piece written by the Icarus Interstellar, an initiative of members of the British Interplanetary Society and the Tau Zero Foundation (TZF) started in 2009: "The title of this blog [Icarus Interstellar] reflects the motivation behind much of what the writer Arthur C. Clarke achieved throughout his life. Reflected in his vision of a positive future for a united humanity in the peaceful exploration of space ... Project Icarus is about more than just designing a vehicle. It is also about keeping the vision of humans in space alive for our generation and the next; a necessary requirement if we are to move forward incrementally towards the stars. For such a vision must be continually renewed if it is to be sustained, matured and eventually achieved. Compatible with this vision are two of the non-technical purposes behind Project Icarus: Firstly, to generate a greater interest in the real-term prospects for interstellar precursor missions that are based on credible science. Second, to motivate a new generation of scientists to be interested in designing space missions that go beyond our solar system. To achieve this requires continuing inspiration and this is how Project Icarus came about."

46   "*Interstellar* 'should be shown in school lessons,'" by Pallab Ghosh, Science correspondent, *BBC News*, June 23, 2015. http://www.bbc.com/news/science-environment-33173197

47   "Dr. Klaus Schwab or: How the CFR Taught Me to Stop Worrying and Love the Bomb," by Johnny Vedmore, *Unlimited Hangout*, March 10, 2022: https://unlimitedhangout.com/2022/03/investigative-reports/dr-klaus-schwab-or-how-the-cfr-taught-me-to-stop-worrying-and-love-the-bomb/

48   "The real legacy of Louis de Rochemont II": http://www.seacoastonline.com/news/20160331/real-legacy-of-louis-de-rochemont-ii

49   Ibid.

50   "Scientist on the Set: An Interview with Marvin Minsky," by David G. Stork, *MIT Press*: https://web.archive.org/web/20071113031417/http://mitpress.mit.edu/e-books/Hal/chap2/two1.html

51 "AI Pioneer Accused of Having Sex with Trafficking Victim on Jeffrey Epstein's Island," by Russell Brandom, *The Verge*, August 9, 2019: https://www.theverge.com/2019/8/9/20798900/marvin-minsky-jeffrey-epstein-sex-trafficking-island-court-records-unsealed
52 http://dangerousminds.net/comments/anthony_burgess_and_the_top_secret_code_in_a_clockwork_orange
53 Lewis' Curzon Street contact claimed "Burgess' collaborator was a former CIA officer called Howard Roman, a languages expert whose particular field had been the Polish Intelligence Service, the Urzad Bezpieczenstwa (UB)—and it was a senior officer in Polish military intelligence, Michal Goleniewski, who upon defecting had told the CIA about the mole at Underwater Weapons Establishment Portland." https://dangerousminds.net/comments/anthony_burgess_and_the_top_secret_code_in_a_clockwork_orange
54 "By 1968, ARPA's patience with Simulmatics was fast running out. In a final hail merry, the company turned to Lansdale acolyte William Godel. Godel had been out of ARPA since 1964. In the intern, he served a prison sentence and ran guns in Southeast Asia. Godel attempted to get Simulmatics a contract in Thailand, where Pool had originally wanted the company to work out of. There, Simulmatics would study the regional police and security forces on behalf of ARPA. But by this time, the agency had had enough of both Simulmatics and Godel and declined the project. Father Hoc and Godel weren't the only Lansdale cronies actively working with the Simulmatics crew by this time either. When Pool toured Vietnam during 1967 as part of Simulmatics' ARPA work, he stayed at the villa of Lansdale groupie Daniel Ellsberg. The two men were already on friendly terms by then. Upon Ellsberg's return from Vietnam, but before his whistleblower escapades, he regularly collaborated with Pool."
55 "Simulmatics Corporation Invented the Future," by Jill Lepore, *New Yorker*, July 27, 2020: https://www.newyorker.com/magazine/2020/08/03/how-the-simulmatics-corporation-invented-the-future
56 The term "cult" first appeared in English in 1617, derived from the French *culte*, meaning "worship," which in turn originated from the Latin word *cultus* meaning "care, cultivation, worship."
57 The reference is to Crowley, who considered his *Book of the Law* to be "the new word of the Aeon."
58 "Disneyland is presented as imaginary in order to make us believe that the rest is real, when in fact all of Los Angeles and the America surrounding it are no longer real, but of the order of the hyperreal and of simulation." *Selected Writings*, Jean Baudrillard, Stanford University Press, 2001.

59 A recent, if frivolous exception, the comedy film *Adventures in Public School*.
60 *Haunted Heart: The Life and Times of Stephen King*, by Lisa Rogak. "I had written *The Shining* without realizing that I was writing about myself."
61 "Kubrick on *The Shining*: An Interview with Michel Ciment," http://www.visual-memory.co.uk/amk/doc/interview.ts.html
62 It's possible to trace central father figures throughout Kubrick's work, from *2001* to *Eyes Wide Shut*. In *2001* there's the Monolith, HAL, and the government which both HAL and Bowman work for. In *A Clockwork Orange*, it's the government that imprisons Alex, rapes his psyche, and then makes "friends" with him at the end. In *Barry Lyndon*, Barry's father is conspicuous by his complete absence (we see him a couple of times but he has no real part in the story, or in Barry's development). Barry's attempt to attain status in high (patriarchal) society can be seen as the son's doomed attempt to receive the paternal blessing he never got. His own stepson hates him and wounds him permanently in the leg. His beloved blood son dies senselessly in a horse-riding accident, at around Danny's age. The drill sergeant in *Full Metal Jacket* is an obvious paternal figure who disciplines his children to be soldiers. Like Yahweh, he programs them to kill (he even has them sing twisted rhymes to cement their allegiance to murder). Lastly, in *Eyes Wide Shut*, Bill Harford is another of Kubrick's fathers, though you would never guess it, since the children are less of a presence than the furniture. Like Barry, Harford is seeking access to the higher echelons of power but is perpetually refused the paternal "blessing." (The Sydney Pollock character is a twisted father figure.) Then there's Kubrick's professed love for *The Godfather*, a film he saw many times and (according to Michael Herr) which he thought was probably the best film ever made. *The Godfather* is seen as the undisputed American classic due, I think, to its flawless depiction of the terrible cost which a corrupt father's legacy has upon the son who tries to live up to it—who gives up his soul (a chance at an individuated psyche) to gain the world (patriarchal power). Kubrick had three daughters, one he adopted when he married his third wife, then two more which they had together. He never sired a son.
63 "Because early traumas are imprinted indelibly in the early fear system—the amygdalan 'psychotic core' of the brain—every detail of traumatic German and Austrian childrearing was restaged during the Holocaust. As Jews were locked into the concentration camps, they were told: 'This is a death camp … You'll be eaten by lice; you'll rot in your own shit, you filthy shitface.' As Germans and Austrians enduring their own filthy swaddling bands as infants, Jews were also made

to live in their own filth, forced to lie in barracks 'awash with urine and feces,' forced to eat their own feces, and finally died in showers 'covered all over with their excrement.' German toilet training was even restaged in precise detail, such as by having the ghetto latrine supervised by a 'guard with a big clock, whom the Germans dressed as a rabbi and called the "shit-master"' ... Even the beating of Jews would often restage the hallowed German practice of insisting that the child not cry out—so the parent wouldn't feel guilty—with Jews in camps being rewarded with some food if they didn't cry out while being beaten by their guards. Every abusive practice of childrearing at the turn of the century that was imprinted in their early fear network, their 'psychotic core,' was released like a time bomb. The Judenfrage was transparently a Kinderfrage restaged." "The Childhood Origins of the Holocaust," speech given by Lloyd deMause on September 28, 2005, at Klagenfurt University, Austria. From the same speech: "Since Jewish mothers almost always breast-fed their babies and since Jewish children were far less authoritarian than their neighbors, Jews were far more liberal as a group than the rest of Germany; for instance, Jews comprised the majority of Viennese Social Democrats. They had to be exterminated to purify the nation; as Goebbels put it, 'The Jews are like the lice of civilized mankind. Somehow they must be exterminated, or they will invariably resume their tormentive [sic] and molesting role,' fearing that Germans were 'about to perish of the Jewish disease.' Himmler expressed the childhood source of the Holocaust similarly: 'Anti-Semitism is exactly like delousing. The removal of lice is not an ideological question, but a matter of hygiene.'" http://primal-page.com/holocaus.htm

64 Ibid.
65 "Did You Know? Philosophy of the Indian Act," http://whitespottedhorse.com/index.php/did-you-know/ Native Americans are more neotenous people, meaning they actually are more "childlike" in a strictly biological sense. (Neoteny is the retention by adults of traits previously seen only in the young. In neoteny, the physiological development is slowed or delayed.) This doesn't mean they were more dependent, however. Women are also more neotenous than men, and Native Americans had been living off the land for centuries before the colonizers arrived and systematically severed that connection to their "mother," making them dependent on the social system instead. At the same time, neoteny could be a factor in the unusually high vulnerability of Natives to alcoholism and drug addiction.
66 The attitude of the American government against the Natives is clearly stated in written documents of William Sherman, a solider,

businessman, and author who served under General Grant in the American Civil War: "We are not going to let a few thieving, ragged Indians check and stop the progress of the railroads ... We must act with vindictive earnestness against the Sioux, even to their extermination, men, women and children. [They must] feel the superior power of the Government." Soldiers should not "pause to distinguish between male and female, or even discriminate as to age." In an 1867 letter to Grant, Sherman even referred to his policy against the native Americans as "the final solution to the Indian problem." http://www.cs.mcgill.ca/~rwest/link-suggestion/wpcd_2008-09_augmented/wp/w/William_Tecumseh_Sherman.htm

67 Hitler biographer John Toland supports this view: "Hitler's concept of concentration camps as well as the practicality of genocide owed much, as he himself claimed, to his studies of British and North American history ... and for the Indians in the Wild West. [He] often praised to his inner circle the efficiency of America's extermination by starvation and uneven combat of the Red Savages 'who could not be tamed by captivity'" (*Adolf Hitler* Vol II, 1976).

68 https://jeffsearle.blogspot.com/2010/12/the-myth-of-theseus-and-minotaur.html

69 Keeping a secret that pertains to a corrupt "father" is something many children are forced to do. Sometimes the secret is kept from the family; probably more often, it is kept by the family. Even something as "simple" as having an alcoholic or adulterous father, in an environment that forbids any mention of it, is a serious betrayal of trust for a child. Such an environment is subtly abusive and cruelly isolating—crazy-making. In order to survive at a crucial stage in which its survival is anything but assured, the child must allow itself to be "co-opted"—to be recruited into a cover-up.

70 Rotman, p. 84.

71 http://faqtheshining.blogspot.ca/2008/08/who-rolls-yellow-ball-to-danny-as-he.html I was looking for a citation about Jack having the shining ability and ended up reading this. It's sort of funny, sort of sad, and sort of fascinating all at the same time. The need to believe. Kubrick shot over 200 hours for *The Shining* (so the record states), so the chances a shitload of continuity errors would end up in the film are spectacularly high. The counter-argument to this is, Kubrick was too much of a genius and a stickler for detail to let it happen. My guess? He knew there'd be a lot of errors and decided to go with it rather than fight it. Placing some deliberate and obvious continuity errors (the vanishing chair behind Jack, magically appearing paper in his typewriter, the changing typewriters) made it *look* like he was doing

it intentionally, as part of the cognitive dissonance effect of a horror movie and as evidence of weird psychic phenomena/shining/the power of the Overlook. Now people are finding every last mistake he made and citing it as evidence for his genius. Now that's genius!

72 "Devolution," from *Taking It All In*, p. 6.

73 "[W]ithin the contemporary digitally enabled scene, a network 'I' is being heralded. The features of such a third, self-enunciating agency, differentiating it from the oral and the scriptive, are becoming discernable. Such an 'I' is *immersive* ... understanding itself as meaningful from without, an embodied agent increasingly defined by the networks threaded through it and experiencing itself, notwithstanding the ubiquitous computer screen interface, as much through touch as vision, through tactile, gestural, and haptic means as it navigates itself through informational space, traversing a 'world of proximity' whose dominant sense is touch. Such an 'I' is *porous*, spilling out of itself, traversed by other 'I's networked to it, permeated by the collectives of other selves and avatars via apparatuses (mobile phone or email, ambient interactive devices, Web pages, apparatuses of surveillance, GPS systems) that form its techno-cultural environment and increasingly break down self-other boundaries thought previously to be uncrossable: what was private exfoliates (is blogged, Webcammed, posted) directly into the social at the same time the social is interjected into the interior of the self, making it 'harder and harder to say where the world stops and the person begins.' Lastly, such an 'I' is *plural* and *distributed* as against the contained, centralized singularity of its lettered predecessor ... In short, a self becoming besides itself, plural, trans-alphabetic, derived from and spread over multiple sites of agency, a self going parallel: a para-self" (Rotman, pp. 8–9). The para-self "is internally heterogeneous and multiple, and, like the computational and imaging technologies mediating it, its behavior is governed by parallel protocols and rhythms—performing and forming itself through many actions and perceptions at once—as against doing or being one thing at a time on a sequential, predominantly endogenous, itinerary." Ibid

74 "In relation to the nature of thought, then, computer science's conversion to parallelism over the past decades amounts to a belated recognition of the presence of collectivities at sites long, deeply, and mistakenly held to be the province of individual, serially thinking subjects." (Rotman, p. 90)

75 "When the symbols are in the environment of the human, and the human is manipulating the symbols, the cognitive properties of the human are not the same as the properties of the system that is made up of the human in interaction with these symbols. The properties

of the human in interaction with the symbols produce some kind of computation that does not mean the computation is happening in the person's head" (Rotman, p. 91).

76 "Digitalization, substituting pixels for points, replaces the psychic architecture and 'metaphysics of interiority' of the Renaissance individual by the architecture that, because it must be specified in relation to the physiologically meaningful substrate of the pixelated image, cannot transcend the space it physically occupies, and so cannot enact a metaphysical drama of viewing the world from a position outside it. [T]he invisible seeing soul has been finally restored to the physiologically sighted body." (Rotman, p. 97)

77 Rotman quotes both Robert Louis Stevenson and Nietzsche on this.

78 "Inside TikTok's Booming Dissociative Identity Disorder Community," by Jessica Lucas, *Input*, July 6, 2021: https://www.inputmag.com/culture/dissociative-identity-disorder-did-tiktok-influencers-multiple-personalities

79 Simply put, the machinery of digital, computer technology is only truly effective as a framework for *an already existing consciousness to emerge through*. Rotman believes that the intelligence that animates the artifact is itself anything but artificial, being innate to physical, biological existence, and even, in a sense, the very basis *of* it—a first cause or organizing principle. Anything less than this and the technology becomes a prison for consciousness—the imposition of *un*consciousness—rather than its apotheosis. The idea of separation between interior and exterior is just that: an idea, a mental construct that, to a quite pervasive degree, creates its own proofs. In fact the inner "I" and the outer collective "fold into each other. All thought, even the most private and enclosed, is from outside itself, socially existing ... using and being used by the media and technological apparatuses that surround us." (Rotman, p, 102). The key principle of the biological and social evolution of individual cognition is its symbiosis with cognitive collectivities and external memory systems, a two-way traffic that allows new cultural formations and technologies of parallelism to reconfigure the thought diagrams inside (as we still say) our heads. "If we are indeed bio-techno-cultural hybrids, if 'nature' is now inseparable from social artifice, and the human is an ongoing, open-ended project of mediated self-construction with shifting boundaries and no identifiable telus, then these directions are not arbitrary or unconditional. Nor do they promise, as many fantasize, a post-human future without death in which digital technology will download minds and at last release psyches from their bodies to float and commune in a sea of disembodied information. Far from escaping embodiment, the action of technology—precisely in the implicit and

unconscious effects of its never absent materiality—is never separable from the bodies of its users, which immediately makes any moving beyond, any attempted abandonment of corporeality, incoherent. From the perspective here the antibody to the illusions of the post-human is the recognition of the para-human, since the condition in question is one of horizontal movement not upwards or forwards but sideways, not linear or sequential but dispersive and parallel, not going beyond, but an expansion, a multiplication, an intensification of what was there, a new realization of the past and its futures and with this a recognition of the incipient plurality of a psyche in the process of becoming beside itself" (Rotman, p. 103).

INDEX

2001: A Space Odyssey (1968), xxii, xxvi, xxvii, 5–6, 7, 13–15, 23, 28, 30–32, 44–45, 47, 48, 49, 56, 57–60, 62, 66–68, 70–71, 79–80, 106, 139, 141–142, 151, 166 (n 62)
    HAL 9000 (character), xx, 13–15, 49, 80, 151, 166 (n 62)
    "Star Gate" VFX sequence from, 6
4chan, xix, 145–147, 149

Abrams, Nathan (film theorist), xxii–xxiii, xxiv, 159 (n 10)
Adam, Ken (production designer), 106
Adam and Eve, 114, 120
AI, xvi, 15, 24, 31, 47–50, 80, 95, 98, 100, 139, 141, 143–148, 150–151, 170–171 (n 79)
    and demonic possession, xii
AI (film), xix, 40
Aldiss, Brian, 163 (n 41)

algorithms (computation), 92–94, 97–101
Allen, Woody
    Kubrick is the anti-, 33
American Film Institute (AFI), 66
Anderson, Paul Thomas, 5, 17
Anger, Kenneth, 78
Anonymous (movement), xxi, 145–146
Apollo 11. *See* Moon-Landing. *See also* Weidner, Jay
Arendt, Hannah, xxii
argument as recreation of a crime scene, 23
ARPA (Advanced Research Projects Agency), 89–92, 165 (n 54)
    ARPANet (internet predecessor), 145–146
artificial intelligence. *See* AI
artists and "the 1%," xxiv
Ascher, Rodney. *See Room 237*
autism, 49, 72, 129

Barry Lyndon (1975), 9, 28, 48, 57, 80, 166 (n 62)
Baudrillard, Jean, 105, 165 (n 58)
Baxter, John (Kubrick biographer), xii, 23, 31–32, 49, 56–58, 74–75, 77–80, 82–83, 161 (n 33), 163 (n 41)
Belson, Jordan (filmmaker), 58
Benson, Michael (author), xxii, 57, 79, 159 (n 11)
Bernstein, Carl, 25–26, 161 (n 29). *See also* Mockingbird
Blacklist, Hollywood, 44
Blavatsky, "Madame" Helena, xix
Blouin ArtInfo (magazine), xvii–xviii
brain-computer interface (BCI), 47, 162 (n 38)
brainwashing, xviii, xxvii, 38
Brando, Marlon, 78–79
Braun, Wernher von, 60
Bremer, Arthur (attempted assassin), 38–39
British Film Institute (BFI), xxiv, 6
British Interplanetary Society (BIS), 60–61, 163–164 (n 44), 164 (n 45)
Buñuel, Luis, 76–77, 87
Burdick, Eugene, 40, 91
Burgess, Anthony, 38, 49, 83–84, 86, 162 (n 39), 165 (n 53)
Burroughs, William S., xv

Cambridge Analytica, 90–92
Cambridge, Project, 90–92
Camelot, Project. *See* ARPA
Cameron, Ewen, 83
Campaign for Nuclear Disarmament (CND), 37
Caras, Roger (press agent), 57
Casey, William J., xxv
Central Intelligence Agency (CIA), 12, 32, 62, 64, 69–70, 73, 124 (n 29), 126 (n 54)
chess, 8, 13–15, 77, 151
cinephilia, the end of, 16–17

Ciment, Michel, 120, 159 (n 6)
Clarke, Arthur C., 13, 15, 31–32, 60–61, 62, 68, 79, 151, 161 (n 33), 164 (n 44, n 45)
  and pedophilia, 60, 163 (n 42)
  humanity's role to create God, 68
Clinton, Hillary, xxvi
Clockwork Orange, A (1971), xii, xiv, xv, xxvi, 7, 14, 20, 28–29, 30, 33, 37–39, 40, 48, 55–56, 57, 71, 77, 81–87, 166 (n 62)
  complements *2001*, 71
  is a meta-movie, 29, 33
ComCom (ARPA project), 90, 92. *See also* Pool, Ithiel de Sola
communists, xxii, xxvii, 44, 91
consensus, being embraced by the, 21
controlled opposition, xxv
Coppola, Francis Ford, 56, 115, 167 (n 62)
Corri, Adrienne, 51, 74, 82
Cosa Nostra, La (LCN). *See* Mafia, American
Cowie, Peter (film historian), 56–57
Critical Race Theory (CRT), xxiv
Cronos (mythological), 114–115, 119, 125
Crowley, Aleister, 78, 98, 139, 165 (n 57)
Cruise, Tom, xiv, xx, xxi, xxiv, 157 (n 2)
Cultural Cold War, The (book). *See* Saunders, Frances Stonor
cult, origin of term, 165 (n 56)
culture
  as fungus, xi–xii
  the problem with, 26
Cumming, Alan, xxiii
Cummings, Alex Sayf, xvii, 16–17, 159

DARPA. *See* ARPA DeBrier, Samson (occultist), 78
deMause, Lloyd (psychohistorian), 122, 127, 130, 166–167 (n 63)

Dick, Philip K., 43, 139
Dissociative Identity Disorder (DID), 148–150
Dr. Strangelove (1964), 5, 7, 29, 30, 40, 44, 56, 57, 68–70, 85, 106, 108
dream of creation, 111
dream-narrative, xii, xv–xvi, xxiii, 161 (30)
dreams, 28, 125, 142, 158–159 (n 4)
  of the author, 43, 140
Douglas, Kirk, 78
Doven, Michael, xiv, xx
Dulles, Allen, 25–26

Eastwood, Clint, 55, 86
emojis, 6
emperor's clothes, xxv–xxvi, 20, 26–27, 40, 72, 88
Epstein, Jeffrey, xvi, 80
Eyes Wide Shut (1999), xi–xxiv, 16, 20, 27, 29, 30, 32, 39, 48, 134, 157 (n 2), 158–159 (n 4), 166 (n 62)

Fabian Society, 37
Fall of Man, 114. See also Adam and Eve
Fargo (TV show), 21
Fauci, Anthony, 95
Fear and Desire (1953), 75, 76–77
fiction aspires to nonfiction, 21–22, 113
Fincher, David, 16, 17
Finn, Ed (media theorist), 93–94, 98
Flying Padre (1951), 75
FOMO (fear of missing out), 100–101
Frewin, Anthony "Tony" (Kubrick assistant), 38, 74
Full Metal Jacket (1987), xiv, 1, 27, 41, 121, 166 (n 64)

genocide, xii, 122, 167–168 (n 66), 168 (n 67). See also Native Americans; Nazis; Residential school system, Canadian
Godel, William, 165 (n 54). See also ARPA
Golden Bough, The (book), 49, 115

Graham, Katharine, 25
Graham, Phil, 25
Gysin, Brion, xv

Harris, James B. (producer), 74, 77–78
Hawley, Noah, 28
Hebb, Donald O., 90
Hinckley, John Jr., 39
history, the lesson of, 23
Hitchcock, Alfred, 6–7, 16, 66, 161–162 (n 36)
Hofstadter, R.J., xvii
Holocaust, Jewish, 9, 40, 122, 166–167 (n 63), 168 (67)
House That Jack Built, The (2018), 97, 137
Hubbard, L. Ron, xx

IBM Corporation, 13, 15, 49
imagination hijacking, 20. See also worshipful fans under Kubrick, Stanley; Kubrickon, the (term)
InfoWars, 10

Jung, Carl, 131

Kafka, Franz, 113, 139
Kahn, Herman (futurist), 56, 59, 69
Kane, Irene, 78
Kael, Pauline, xi, xiii, xvi, xxvi, 20, 28, 31, 32, 38, 55, 56, 58–59, 69, 82, 86, 114–115, 126, 128
Kearns, Juli, 123, 159–160 (n 14). See also Room 237
Kidman, Nicole, xiv, xvii–xviii, xxiv, 157 (n 3), 158–159 (n 4)
Killer's Kiss (1955), 78
Killing, The (1956), 7, 43, 78
King, Stephen, 29, 36, 41, 47, 105, 106, 115, 117, 120, 127, 130–132, 135, 142, 148, 166 (n 60)
Kolker, Robert P. (critic). See Abrams, Nathan.
KUBARK, 66
Kubrick, Christiane, 39, 84, 89

Kubrick, Stanley
  Aryan Papers, The (unfinished project) by, 40
  demanded inauthenticity, xxiii–xxiv
  emotionlessness of the films of, xvi, 4, 85
  father figures in the films of, 53–54, 117, 166 (n 62). *See also* Cronos
  films empty of unconscious matter, 18, 29–30, 73, 151
  films of are impersonal and ultra-personal, 27–28, 33, 45, 125
  films of as cognitively impairing, xxii–xxiii, xxvi–xxvii, 16–17, 45
  films of as desensitization-inducing, 161–162 (n 36)
  films of as hermetic ritual, 7
  films of as intentionally bad, xiv–xv, xviii, 32
  films of as lure for human consciousness, 20, 23–24, 39, 45–46, 47–48, 111, 134, 138
  films of as self-worship, 5–6, 32–33
  films of as vehicles for audience projection, xv–xvi, 5–6, 16, 28, 30
  final speech of, 40
  flying lessons, 75
  litigation against critics, 56–57
  male cult of, 19, 35, 159–160 (n 14)
  "Napoleon" (unfinished project) by, 40–42, 71
  non-submersible sequences film theory of, 23
  operates like an intelligence agent, 74. *See also* Stanley's Irregulars
  overrated, 4, 29, 45, 57
  personal pathologies of, 6–7, 53–54, 78–80, 163 (n 41)
  reduces everyone to slaves, 79–80
  still fooling 'em, 39
  vampire of people's brains, 51, 74
  worshipful fans, xxvi, 6, 17, 19, 20, 26–28, 32

Kubrick, Vivian, 5, 9–10, 20–21, 123. *See also* Scientology, Church of
Kubrickanalia, 140
Kubrickon, the (concept), 39, 46–48, 50, 72, 82, 88, 98, 101, 105, 129, 133, 134, 138, 140, 141, 145
  definition of, 101
  silver key to, 133
  third phase of, 47–48

language restricts perception, 138
Lansdale, Edward, 91, 165 (n 54)
Lethem, Jonathan, 20
Lewis, Roger. *See* Burgess, Anthony
Licklider, J. C. R. "Lick," 90, 92
liminality, 35–36, 40, 46, 109, 132, 141
Lolita (1962), xviii, 44, 78
Look (magazine), 59–60, 75
Luce, Henry (magazine publisher), 26, 66, 76, 78

Mafia, Italian American, 74
magic, 14–15, 45, 50, 68, 96–98, 115
  writing as, 110–111
Margolus, Norman (computer scientist), 143
Maternal psychic bondage (MPB), 106
matrix, 48, 97, 100, 106, 133–134, 144
  second matrix, xxii, 35–36, 45–46, 88. *See also* second womb
Matrix, The (film), 133
May Day, 39
McGregor, Ewan, 21
memeplexes, xxvii, 23, 62
memes, xix, 10, 13, 21, 24, 62, 70–71, 147
Miller, Laura (critic), 19
Minotaur (mythological), 39, 107–109, 123–124, 130
Minsky, Marvin, 27, 80
Miscavige, David, xiv, 157 (n 3)
mistakes are evidence for genius, 162 (n 39), 168–169 (n 71)
MKULTRA, xvii, xx, 78, 85, 86, 90
Mockingbird (Operation), 25–26, 66, 76, 78
Modine, Matthew, 121

INDEX 177

Monarch (Project), xvii–xx. *See also* MKULTRA
Moon-Landing, 8–10, 20, 28, 40, 44, 46, 48, 67, 105–106, 124, 125. *See also* Weidner, Jay
mother is space, and the, 54
Museum of Modern Art (MoMA), 76

National Aeronautics and Space Administration (NASA), 59–60, 66, 70, 80. *See also* Apollo 11
Native Americans, 8, 122–123, 130, 167 (n 65), 167–168 (n 66), 168 (n 67)
Nazis, xxii, 8, 60, 122–123, 130, 137, 166–167 (n 63), 168 (n 67). *See also* genocide
Neuro-linguistic programming (NLP), 35, 43
   neuro-cinematic programming (NCP), 45
Nicholson, Jack, 6, 9, 27, 40, 41, 120, 128, 161 (n 30)
   hyper-real performance, 161 (n 30)
Nolan, Christopher, 16, 17, 61

O'Brien, Cathy, xvii. *See also* Monarch
Obama, Barack, xxvi
occultism, 8, 45, 47, 78, 95, 97–98 *See also* magic
Office of the Coordinator of Inter-American Affairs (OCIAA)

pandemic, COVID-19, xii, 95. *See also* vaccines, mRNA
para-self, 148–150, 152, 169 (n 73)
paranoid style. *See* Hofstadter, R.J.
Paths of Glory (1957), 7, 43, 78, 80
Peckinpah, Sam, 79, 139
pedophilia, xvii, xix, xxv, 44, 60, 163 (n 42)
Peter Pan, 127
Plato, xvii, 142
pluralized self. *See* para-self
Poe, Edgar Allan

mathematical principles informed the poetry of, 24
Polanski, Roman, 4, 139
Pool, James (author), 123
Pool, Ithiel de Sola, 91–92, 165 (n 54)
porno shop excursion, 29, 81–82
Positif (film magazine). *See* Vachaud, Laurent
possession by mother, 106–109, 125, 132–135
post-truth, 22, 25, 96–97, 152
primary wound, 108, 119–135
propaganda derangement syndrome, xxvi
psychism, 41, 118, 131. *See also* shining; telepathy

QAnon, xxi, xxv

Raphael, Frederic, xv
Rathbun, Marty, 157 (n 3)
Residential school system, Canadian, 123. *See also* Native Americans
Richter, Dan (choreographer), 5–6, 159 (n 11)
Rochemont, Richard de, 75–76
Roman, Howard (CIA officer), 165 (n 53)
Room 237 (film), 8–9, 12, 16–17, 28, 39–41, 122–126, 132, 137, 152, 159–160 (n 14)
Rosenman, Leonard (composer), 80
Rotman, Brian, 109, 127, 141–152
Rubicon (river), 139
Ryan, John Fell, 12, 125–126, 130, 160 (n 23)

Saturn (mythological), 114, 121. *See also* Cronos
Saunders, Frances Stonor, 25, 76
Savile, Jimmy, xvi, 83
scapegoating. *See* Halloran, Dick under *Shining, The*
Schnitzler, Arthur, xviii. *See also* traumnovelle (term)
Schrader, Paul, 39
Schwab (blogger), 24

Schwab, Klaus, 69, 70, 143
scientism, xii, 70, 93–95, 97–99, 101
Scientology, Church of, xiv, xx–xxi, 10, 145–146, 157 (n 3)
Scorsese, Martin, xiv, 6, 78, 81
second womb, 47, 133–134
sentience, xvi, xxvii, 48, 49, 111, 134, 151, 152
    the problem Stanley Kubrick devoted his life to solving, 48–49
Shaviro, Steven, 141
shining (concept), 118, 128–130, 131–134, 138, 168 (n 71)
Shining, The (1980), xix–xx, xxii, 8–9, 12, 16–17, 19–20, 27, 29, 32, 38, 40–42, 43, 58, 85, 105, 106, 107–109, 114–115, 119–135, 140, 148, 149, 152, 157 (n 2), 160 (n 22), 161 (n 30, n 32), 161–162 (n 36), 166 (n 62), 168–169 (n 71)
    as coded confession, 9, 28, 105–106, 124
    Hallorann, Dick (character), 41, 43, 126, 128–129
    cornerstone of Kubrickon, 138
    hedge maze from, 42, 62, 123, 126, 127–128, 130, 133
    Overlook Hotel, the, xiv–xix, 8, 27, 39, 41–43, 50, 62, 105, 112, 120, 122–123, 126, 128, 129, 130, 132–134, 137, 140, 148, 162 (n 36), 168–169 (n 71)
Shining, The (novel), 120–121, 132, 135, 166 (n 60)
Sigal, Clancy (writer), 79
Simulmatics Corporation (data science firm). *See* ARPA
Singer, Alexander (filmmaker), 75, 77
Skinner, B.F., 90
smartphones, 100, 142
Snider, Steven William "Recluse" (researcher), 90–92
Snopes, 21

Southern, Terry, 5
space propaganda, 59–61, 66–68, 70–71
Spartacus (1960), 7, 44, 55–56, 74, 78
Spielberg, Steven, 25, 40–41
Stanley Kubrick's Boxes (film), 38
Stanley's Irregulars, 38, 46–47. *See also* operates like an intelligence agent under Kubrick, Stanley
Stevens, George, 66
Stevens, George Jr., 66
Streep, Meryl, 25
Strieber, Whitley, 129, 131, 138, 139
superculture, xxv

taste (aesthetic), social formation of, xi–xii
telepathy, 47, 129
theses of this work, two primary, 24
TikTok, 149
time, 107, 114–115, 120, 122, 126, 137. *See also* Cronos
Time (magazine). *See* Luce, Henry
transgenderism, xxiv
trauma, 112, 121–123, 133–134, 138, 148–150, 166–167 (n 63). *See also* deMause, Lloyd; MKULTRA; Monarch
traumnovelle (term), 13, 134. *See* Schnitzler, Arthur for novella
trivium and quadrivium, 24
Trump, Donald, xxv–xxvi

unconsciousness, imposition of, 170–171 (n 79)
Upton, Charles, 96–97
United States Information Agency (USIA), 63–67

vaccines, mRNA, xxvi–xxvii, 99
Vachaud, Laurent, xvi–xxi, 159 (n 6, n 10)
violence, screen, 28–29, 37–39, 55–56, 83, 85–86
Vitali, Leon, 9

Watchmen (comic), 39, 134
Weidner, Jay, xvii, 9, 28, 40, 41, 46, 105, 124–125. *See also Room 237*
Welles, Orson, 73, 75–76, 78
Wells, H.G., 75
White, Armond, 16–17
Who Paid the Piper? (book). *See* Saunders, Frances Stonor
Wilder, Billy, 6, 66
Wisner, Frank (CIA co-founder), 32

word vs. image, 117, 127–128, 129, 132–133, 142
World Assembly of Youth (1952 US Department of State film), 75
World Economic Forum (WEF), 69–70, 90

Yahweh, 117, 120, 127, 129, 166 (n 62)

Žižek, Slavoj, xv, 27, 158–159 (n 4)

Coming soon, the follow-up to *The Kubrickon*:
Big Mother: The Technological Body of Evil

Contents:
Introduction: Womb envy

Part I: Neurodiversity & Philip K. Dick's no name entities
1. Your real imaginary friend
2. Intense world syndrome/autists as receiver-transmitters
3. Consciousness + biology ÷ trauma = culture & technology?
4. Alien Signals (*2001* & *Blade Runner*: autism, ai, & empathy)
5. Autist time-slip
6. Lost prophets
7. The other side
8. Sci-Fi author seeks novel to live in
9. How am i not myself?

Part II: Transgender & the rise of the dream-state
10. *The Matrix* meets dominatrix
11. Body dysphoria, autism, crypto-eugenics
12. The madness of the many: sex education by Baron Munchausen
13. Transhumanism: the ultimate in unmentionable obscenity
14. A verbal universe

Part III: Artificial mind
15. Philip K. Dick & the counterfeit
16. Sins against soma: entheogens & the structural reality of the body
17. The anti-plasmate
18. Tech-gnosticism unborn
19. The serial killer vs. the people: the techniques of satanism
20. Satan's boomerang: monsters, heroes, and victims
21. Internal abusers & ai: autists & psychopaths meet evil halfway
22. King Batty (who has more children in his basement: Sam Harris or Ted Bundy?)
23. God's original dialectic

Appendix: Scientism

www.ingramcontent.com/pod-product-compliance
Ingram Content Group UK Ltd.
Pitfield, Milton Keynes, MK11 3LW, UK
UKHW021612220126
467229UK00012B/307